TO THE
WORKPLACE

HOW AN AWESOME ATTITUDE AND
A PEPPY PERSPECTIVE WILL HELP YOU GO,
FIGHT AND WIN AT WORK!

MELINDA
CARTER OAKES

The material in this publication is of the nature of general comment only and does not represent professional advice. It is not intended to provide specific guidance for particular circumstances and it should not be relied on as the basis for any decision to take action or not take action on any matter which it covers. Readers should obtain professional advice where appropriate before making any such decision. To the maximum extent permitted by law, the author and publisher disclaim all responsibility and liability to any person, arising directly or indirectly from any person taking or not taking action based on the information in this publication.

Westwind, LLC
118 Monell Street
Penn Yan, NY 14527

The Cheerleader's Guide to the Workplace
How an Awesome Attitude and a Peppy Perspective Can Help You Go, Fight and Win in the Workplace

ISBN: 979-8-218-26842-8 Paperback
ISBN: 979-8-218-26843-5 Ebook

Cover and Interior Design by KUHN Design Group | kuhndesigngroup.com

Editing by Lisa Howard

Dedicated to Brett—my base.
Also to my fellow Lions and Wildcats.

CONTENTS

PREFACE

When I decided to write this book, I went all in—I put myself and my intentions on the centerline for everyone to see. I shared my idea broadly and interviewed many of my former teammates to gain perspectives and quite frankly to set expectations for all of us. In cheerleading, when you tell your teammates and partners that you're going to "go" on the next eight-count, you better go! If you don't, you can cause a major breakdown in your team's ability to reach their collective goals, and without question, you'll miss your own chance, too. It's the same in the workplace.

To grow in any career capacity, you have to put yourself out there. You have to set expectations for yourself and you have to be open and accountable to and for others. It also helps to know what the moves are and work your way through the trenches, trying out new things *and* old things while you gain confidence and credibility.

One of the many things I've learned as I worked *my* way to my definition of success is that the slow road is actually the scenic road. Taking your time to work through the layers and levels of your career doesn't stunt your growth—rather, it prepares you to be catapulted or "tossed to hands," as I like to say. It's a badge of honor to know, intimately, the ins and outs of a job. It's also the best way to gain experience and become an expert and ultimately an ambassador. But it's not all about you.

The Cheerleader's Guide to the Workplace offers more than just cheers and encouragement as you tread your personal path to happiness and productivity! It also explains how to lift others up as you go. If you haven't already learned this for yourself, you'll see through the examples I provide why it's just as important to be the partner—the colleague at work who's cheering for everyone else, building alliances and cultivating that team spirit—as it is to jump up at every opportunity. If you don't already know that someone is cheering for you as you go about your day, know that I am! If you could use a pocket-sized pep squad, consider this the book for you.

TRYOUTS

JUDGMENT

*"I think it's awfully hard to prepare yourself
for an entire year for something that you
do for five minutes. It's a lot of pressure."*

ALLISON WEIL, THE UNIVERSITY OF ALABAMA

recall two occasions when I participated in media training workshops. They reminded me of cheerleading tryouts because you had
to perform at the top of your game for a singular or even nonexis-
tent audience. It's incredibly awkward and unnerving. If you've never
experienced an official tryout or media training session, perhaps you
can relate to the feeling of making good on a dare proposed by your
wildest, most fearless friend or interviewing for a dream job when
you know there are 50 other candidates. In all of those cases, everyone is looking for one thing: the screwup. You can nail 99.9% of
the moment, but if you say one single "Umm" or blink awkwardly,
you're outta there!

The media training workshops were relatively rigorous and definitely thorough. They took place roughly two years apart, while I

was employed by the same company. My colleagues and I were working to improve and perfect our craft as on-camera spokespeople for one of the world's largest and most beloved consumer products companies, and our presentation of the brand was important to us. We loved the company as well as the products we represented…and of course, we also wanted to keep our jobs. There were hundreds if not thousands of people who would've gladly jumped into our roles if we had failed to make the cut.

In advance of the training, the consultants memorized our personal bios: where we'd gone to school, what we studied, what we liked to do in our free time, all of the details. We even had to tell them in advance what we thought our on-camera weaknesses were so they could poke extra hard in those areas. They also researched our company and its products and programs, although we were intentionally left to wonder what questions they would ask us while the cameras were rolling. Little neophyte me, I thought the goals were strictly to see if we had any speech nuances or physical mannerisms that would distract from our message and if we could stay on point with calm confidence when counterpoints were made to our answers.

I won't try to convince you that I felt calm in front of the cameras back then or that I feel calm now, even after years of practice in front of various formats of listeners. I simply don't. In fact, despite the fact that I really enjoy and look forward to public speaking opportunities, my heart races unbearably fast, I have an unfounded desire to use the ladies room, and I find myself having deep, deep inner dialogues about breathing slowly, blinking slowly, loosening up my shoulders and looking as chill as possible and casually indifferent to the moment…but also appearing to be generally approachable. I'll also share that I have a terrible habit of memorizing my speeches, which leaves little room for a natural conversational-style presentation. Sometimes I assume my punchlines will work and I even write a "pause for laughter" moment into my speeches. Sometimes the line doesn't land, but then I just use that time to take a little pause for my own internal nervous laughter. Either way, it usually works out. For the most part.

While I'm not setting the public speaking world on fire, I'm also not going down in flames. Perhaps I've inadvertently used the same adjective two or three times in a segment or never mentioned the company I worked for by name (just sayin', it might have happened once or twice…), but I always make my one key point. At least, that's *my* assessment of the situation. But there's always another one: the viewer's. If someone is a member of your personal hype club, they're going to think you did an *amazing* job 100% of the time. That's how love works. Full support! However, if your viewer is someone who doesn't know you and is strictly looking to be informed, criticisms are sure to pop up.

In a perfect world, it's about the content of your conversation. In the real world, it's more often about you. In the case of my media training experience, the viewers were the media trainers, and they absolutely and positively had no affinity for me—they were there only to judge my presentation, which consisted both of the content and me.

The way I see it, the interesting and tricky thing about being judged is the way it relates to the zodiac sign Gemini. Some people believe that Gemini represents a person who is two-faced, and that's technically true—Gemini literally has two faces that can see in different directions and with different perspectives. In this same manner, judgment can be both objective, which is what I was expecting out of media training (looking at the content), and also subjective, which is not what I was expecting (looking at me). I always forget about the latter. I like to imagine that we walk around our world using specific criteria for identifying very objective strengths and opportunities, but the reality is that we don't. It's okay, though—you just have to know that and be prepared. If you *are* prepared, you can and will outshine, surprise and delight those who stand in objective *or* subjective judgment.

As it turned out, I did a good job in both media training sessions. I could not be distracted from my key message points. I was calm and pleasant. I appeared knowledgeable about my subject matter. I engaged in appropriate conversation and eye contact. I maintained a good posture and presence. I checked off all the major boxes for public speaking…except one, that is. It's a funny one. It's the subjective one that used to always catch me off guard. It's one I've missed the mark on more or less since birth (or realistically, since I was about two years old) and definitely all through junior high and high school. It plagued me roughly until I turned 40 and said "To heck with it!" Truly, the topic comes up even to this day, although I no longer mind. I'm over it. I embrace it. I actually love it. That one thing is…my hair.

"You might just want to control it somehow—maybe wear it straight or put it back," said one consultant, sounding much like the another one. "It's really…big. And full. I mean, it's beautiful and people would love to have that much hair…it's just a bit distracting on camera…"

I have naturally big and curly hair. It's not so much thick as there's just a lot of it. My adorable mom has stick-straight hair and my dad, a retired career Army officer, has never had a single hair longer than half an inch. Growing up, nobody—including me—really knew what to do with my hair other than cut it.

So there I sat, unprepared for the feedback. And when I received it, instead of thinking about it objectively, I took it personally, because that's how we roll as we're growing up and developing our prefrontal cortex, trying to get all adulty and stuff.

And that's why I'm writing this book. If I've learned one thing from my hair's journey through time, I've learned that life and the workplace are objective *and* subjective and we need to be prepared for both. Feedback can be both professional and personal. Taken with a grain of salt and an open mind, that can be okay. If you don't grow from the constructive feedback specifically, you might just grow from the self-discovery or healing process of hearing something you don't like and managing your way through it. Something like "You didn't make the cut because you weren't X [sharp enough/loud enough/flashy enough]." Or "You weren't a team player" or "You didn't embrace your unique talents enough." Or "Your hair is really out of control and distracting." It happens to all of us, so we all need to be prepared.

Once I realized that criticism and negativity are directly related to an individual's own perceptions and their relationship to the subject matter, I realized that I could take the best of other people's intentions and leave the worst behind and continue moving forward. That's a mindset of positivity and forward momentum. You know who else had that mindset? Thomas Edison. The famous inventor was once asked how it felt to fail 1,000 times before the lightbulb worked. Edison replied, "I didn't fail 1,000 times. The light bulb was an invention with 1,000 steps." Brilliant response.

In advance of my media training, I thought I was going to be evaluated on the content and delivery of my speaking points, which is to say on my ability to perform my *actual job*. But that's just it. That's the point. I made the mistake of thinking that my job was something other than me, when in fact the tasks of the job and the person performing it go together just like Gemini. They're a two-part whole. They're inseparable.

And that two-for-one deal is how you end up working with a person who has the best personality but is "all sizzle and no steak." That's how you end up working with a person who's incredibly smart but a lackluster people-person. It really *does* take all types in the workplace. And we should strive to be the best of both the objective and the subjective.

You've heard the phrase "You are what you eat," right? Well, you're also what you do: mind, body and spirit. And guess what? I've got the spirit, yes I do. I've got the spirit, how about you? Let me just go ahead and answer that question now and say "Yes! Yes, you *do* have spirit and it's as fabulous as everyone else's! It's just…yours."

When I think of the mind-body-spirit connection, I like to think the mind part is objective, the body part is subjective and the spirit part is…well, that comes down to your specialty. My spirit specialty looks a lot like a string of gingerbread people because I'm a connector of people and ideas. From the outside, Thomas Edison's spirit looks to me like perseverance. (Although what I wouldn't give to know what *he* would say was his spirit specialty!) Maybe your specialty looks like arriving early, being consistently dependable, leaving a "Good job!" note on a colleague's desk, responding with lightning speed to emails and requests, helping seasoned colleagues with technical upgrades without making them feel outdated, sharing earned and learned wisdom, listening more than you talk or talking to everyone in every capacity within your company. Any way you spin it, spirit—just like in cheerleading—is the special sauce.

So the next time you receive objective or subjective feedback that's at odds with your expectations or the person judging you has a weak point of view or an adverse relationship with the subject matter, harness your inner spirit and take that feedback just like Thomas Edison did: as a confirmation of a multi-step work in progress. Then go shine brightly!

BUCKETS & CANDLESTICKS

"I think it's important to reach out to people you otherwise wouldn't normally talk to and just give them a compliment. Say 'You're doing an awesome job and I appreciate you. I couldn't do my job successfully without you.'"

OMAYRA DEHRING, KANSAS STATE UNIVERSITY

n cheerleading, there are hand positions. There are jazz hands (you know 'em, you love 'em!), blades (I always thought *Blades of Glory*, the 2007 movie starring Will Ferrell, would've been better if it had been about cheerleading) and fists, which is the more common hand position. Within the category of fists, there are candlesticks and buckets. I realize I'm in the cheerleading weeds here and this is not really a book about cheerleading, but candle-stick with me.

Imagine you're holding a candle in your hand in an upright position so that it burns correctly and you don't get covered with drips of scalding hot wax the way you might have if you've ever experienced midnight mass on Christmas Eve while singing "Silent Night."

Perfect. That is the "candlestick" position. Conversely, fists facing the ground in such a way that you could be holding the handle of a slop bucket are "bucket" fists. Really, the positions are brilliantly named, but how does this relate to you in the workplace, you ask? It relates because it's a metaphor for the little things. Literally it's a quarter turn of the wrist, but when I see a candlestick that should be or could be a bucket, I notice.

Little things are not small things. Little things matter. For example, little things matter when it comes to how you structure your time. How often have you said or felt that you just didn't have enough time to get everything done that you needed to get done? The reason is a piddly excuse for most of us—according to the Pew Research Center, "44% of 18- to 49-year-olds say they go online almost constantly" (Perrin and Atske, 2021). *Tsk, tsk.* I'm definitely judging us, but in an objective sort of way because I'm using hard facts and calculations. Also, how many times have you heard that we make time for what's important to us? I'm going to go ahead and say probably a lot, because I just stuck that phrase into a Google search and received 14.3 billion results in 0.66 seconds. No, really. Try it.

Okay, okay…so we know we spend too much time on our phones and by default experience a deficit of time spent on things that perhaps should be more important to us. Now, I'm not going to drone on and on about how there's a bit of a misnomer here because that cute little meme about "quality time" doesn't necessarily take into account some bigger issues like addiction and—wait for it—nomophobia. (It's a real thing and an actual word. Look it up! …On your phone for irony.) So let's table that conversation and instead talk about the little things you can do that are related to time management and that will give you a leg up in the workplace.

Almost universally, experts agree that the first thing you need to do to better manage your time is understand how you currently *spend* your time and then set goals around how you'd like to improve that spending to make the most and best of yourself. Personally, I find that setting tiny little goals is the key to success with respect to time management. For example, after years of claiming that I didn't have enough time to work out, I decided to wake up five minutes earlier each day, and then, instead of giving myself grace to scroll through Instagram and Pinterest until the snooze alarm sounded 10 minutes later, I would spend the now 15 minutes with my virtual trainers. Guess what? That five-minute tweak worked! And it's been such a sweet little win that I crave more little wins just like it. So likewise, instead of spending the last waking moments of my day saying a virtual goodnight to all of my friends and their happy Facebook stories, I read a motivational, historical fiction or nonfiction book. Sometimes I only make it through one page before my eyelids become too heavy, but it's a win that fills me with a little extra enthusiasm for my next day. I'll take it.

The other thing you need to keep in mind when managing your time is to prioritize your must-do items. One of my favorite authors is the immortal Mark Twain. On time management, he allegedly said, "If it's your job to eat a frog, it's best to do it first thing in the morning. And if it's your job to eat two frogs, it's best to eat the biggest one first." I can't even begin to tell you how much I love that quote or how many times I've used it since I first discovered it, but suffice to say, it's a lot! One of my friends even suggested a take on that quote for the title of this book. It's so juicy! The quote, not the frog. With that quote in mind, let's jump right back into the main points of this chapter.

For several years during my career in the consumer products industry, I had the responsibility of providing licensing partners with anticipated and actual sales numbers from every country in the world. This was a daunting task, because at the time, the company I worked for didn't plan sales at the country level but rather at the regional level. Extracting and validating the information I needed was, in short, a frog. But like Mark Twain advised, in order to get the information I needed from colleagues around the world in different time zones, mornings were the best option for getting that work done. Coupled with a fresh cup of coffee and a few Excel shortcuts, I ate that frog for breakfast at least once a quarter for six years. *Ribbit.*

Moving on from frogs and the importance of time management, seeing as time is money, let's apply the "little things matter" theory to just that, money. Have you heard of compound interest? Bad if you're talking about your loan, good if you're talking about your savings. Let's take the positive narrative of savings as an example of compound interest. Say that when you graduated from high school or college, you received a total of $1,000 as graduation gifts. You deposited all of that in a savings account. Let's apply the historical market return rate after inflation for the past 30 years: about 7.25%. (Not bad!) Let's also say that you've been adding $50 each month to your initial deposit. After 30 years, you'll have $73,239. Compare that with what you would have had 30 years later if you hadn't added anything to the initial $1,000: a total of $8,747. If you did add the monthly contribution of $50 but there was no compounding interest, in 30 years, that savings account would have $19,000. Compound interest is a little thing, but it makes a very big difference. (If the preceding paragraph was as much fun for you as it was for me, check out www.nerdwallet.com to create your own savings roadmap.)

But! A big but. As encouraging as our savings example is, keep in mind that interest rates can work *against* you! Instead of the $1,000 being in your savings account, imagine that it's on your credit card. In 2023, the average credit card interest rate hit 24%. If for some reason you fall into financial hardship and pay nothing on your credit card "loan," it would take fewer than three years for your debt to *double*. See, time isn't the only thing that goes by too quickly!

Little things matter with time, and little things matter with money. Little things also matter in the way you think and how you reflect. In fact, reflection and metacognition are incredibly important and indeed necessary for you to do in order to evaluate actions you previously took. They're also crucial to do in order to be better prepared to face similar situations in the future and take ever-improving actions. This is exactly the type of judgment that *isn't* such a bad thing! It's also the wise step to take to be prepared for that unanticipated feedback we talked about in the last chapter.

If you've read the book *Choose Your Story, Change Your Life* by Kindra Hall, you know it's a great read. If you haven't read it, my hyper Cliff's Notes version of the book is that you need to create positive narratives around your experiences and your goals. Exhibit A: that's exactly what I did when I decided to write this book. I said, "Melinda. You are not all sizzle and no steak. You can totally do this! You have a lot of ideas you've followed through on. You've experienced feelings of success and you've learned a lot from doing and watching. This book is yours for the making. Now give it a try!"

This positive narrative creation process relates to something with a fancy name in the psychological research world: "emotion regulation." More specifically, it's a part of emotion regulation that happens even before the emotion occurs (called "reappraisal"). It's a strategy that's "aimed at modifying the emotional meaning and impact of a situation" (Gross and John, 2003).

You might be thinking that it sounds like I have peanut butter in my mouth and wondering how on earth you regulate an emotion *before* it even happens, but wonder no more! Part of the answer to how you pre-regulate goes back to what we talked about in the previous chapter, namely a judgment alerting you to the fact that you need to be prepared for both objective *and* subjective feedback in certain situations. But you also need to continuously evaluate the actions you're taking and the responses you're giving so that when something similar happens again, you're ready. This is a little thing that you can do while you're eating your lunch, commuting to and from work, taking a shower, talking with your favorite person, or drifting off to sleep. It's a little thing, but it's significant! It will go a long way towards creating a more positive state of well-being.

And while you're thinking positive things, don't just think about your *own* things—think about other people within your sphere of influence, too. We've already talked about how little things matter in relation to time and money, but we're going to add one more big little thing to our list: how we treat others. Little things matter in a really, really big way when it comes to how we treat others. You already know that's true, but it's worth reminding ourselves about. While we're busy setting our personal goals and working towards becoming the best versions of ourselves, we need to be aware that our personal development is happening in an environment that nearly always includes others. Even during the lockdown era, we still generally encountered others in the workplace in the form of our bosses, our peers, our subordinate colleagues and everyone else who makes the workplace hum. This constant state of interacting with others (online or offline) means that you don't just need to reflect on your own actions, you should reflect on the actions of others, too, so that you can respond with kindness, mindfulness and resilience to their actions as well as your own. Doing so also helps create a mindset of learning and appreciation instead of envy or anger.

The *Greater Good Magazine* (www.greatergood.berkeley.edu) posted a terrific read on this very topic in an article written by Emiliana Simon-Thomas in August of 2018. The article, titled "The Four Keys to Happiness at Work" is about, well, happiness at work. Such a perfect title for the topic! I recommend perusing it a time or two or three! Simon-Thomas offers a lot of important learnings, but as it relates to this chapter, I'm going to focus on mindfulness, or real-time awareness. That, Simon-Thomas says, in the third of the four keys, will help with "reversing our learned habits of self-criticizing or blaming others."

Reflecting on the number of times I've blamed others for any number of small or large infractions or mishaps, I feel even more determined to use this opportunity to encourage you to stop doing what I did and start doing more reflecting and real-time thinking so that you don't have to wait decades to learn their benefits like I did. Mindfulness not only helps us positively evaluate ourselves, it also helps us be more present with others. A quick search at the bookstore or online will cultivate several "Top Ten" lists of ways to be more mindful, but no matter which list you read, you'll find that listening is essential. Slow down, look people in the eyes when they're talking and hear what they're saying—you'll start to become more mindful and more aware of what's driving their narrative.

In my own workplace journey, I struggled with this for years because I always heard any negative comment as being a personal criticism and I saw the person delivering those comments as working against me. We'll talk more about criticism and feedback in the Listen, Coach chapter, but for now, I'll share that there was one day when my opinion on feedback did a full 180-degree turn. Amidst the most stunning display of mindfulness I've ever witnessed, a senior leader at a company I worked for was under intense verbal fire from a buyer at a key retail account. By "intense," I mean there were definitely bits of spittle flying through the air, beads of sweat on all visible skin surfaces, frazzled hairs, a red (if not purple) face and clenched fists. There was possibly an inhaler thrown into the mix that might or might not have been mine, but then again, I could have slightly inflated the weight of the moment in my mind over time. Either way, it was volcanic. It was like a stereotypical scene in a play.

I wasn't the target of the rage, but it came on the heels of my presentation and I was physically near it. It felt personal; my adrenaline was definitely pumping. I knew the buyer wanted to hear from the highest-ranking person in the room, and for once, I was very glad that wasn't me. It honestly wasn't even *close* to being me. Had I been responsible for the response, I would have definitely fumbled it…and that would have happened even *after* having had to take a couple of deep puffs from the aforementioned inhaler. Thankfully, our VP of sales was a seasoned professional and I had the chance to watch the coolest, most collected and clearly mindful response I'd ever seen unfold.

Cue the four-step process. First, there was intense listening. Second, there was a…pause…before the response came. I've since learned that pausing gives us a moment to think, process our thoughts and most importantly calm ourselves and be less reactive. (As a side benefit, I'm convinced it gives the aggressor a moment to calm themselves down, too.) Third, there was a validation of the concerns that had been expressed. Fourth and finally, a few options for moving forward were suggested, both immediate options and long-term options. Those ensuing suggested solutions may seem so basic and easy, but emotions definitely get in the way of making *anything* easy. I was flabbergasted in a good way.

What I learned from my immediate reflection was that first and foremost, I always need to be developing my skills. It's good to be in close proximity to more experienced, more mindful and very talented individuals! The aggressive buyer was under incredible pressure from his own workplace; within a year, his company would go bankrupt and liquidate its stores. By thinking about that event over (and over) over time, whenever I see a bigger moment unfold (albeit one that's usually less emotional), I perceive that it's not at all about me. Such moments have become much more understandable. Now when I experience what seems to be an overreaction in the workplace, my knee-jerk emotion is wonder—I wonder what's happening in their work life or personal life that has amplified the moment, and I wonder what part I can play to make the situation better.

That example of the buyer was a little moment in time—maybe fewer than two minutes, in actuality—but it wasn't a small moment. It has stayed with me to this day, and it occurred in 2007! So it was little, but it wasn't small. Little things are never small.

STANDING OUT

"I don't think you ever allow yourself to play
small just so other people feel comfortable.
It doesn't matter what the situation is, you
always have to play it big because you
don't know who you're inspiring."

CAROLINE NASH, GEORGIA SOUTHERN UNIVERSITY

id you know that every year since 2001, March 1st has had the
distinction of being World Compliment Day? How amazing is
that? And why didn't I already know that? Compliments travel
straight to our soul and make themselves at home, fueling our spirit
like gas/electricity in a car. At the risk of rehashing the scientific com-
plexity of emotion regulation, I'll tell you that compliments not only
feel good thanks to the neurotransmitter dopamine, they also play
an important role in moving us forward in a task-oriented manner,
something that's critical in the workplace. Clearly, being recognized
is an important part of the whole career experience. That said, compliments themselves require some amount of delicacy. Christopher
Littlefield, an employee appreciation specialist, has said that although

"the number one thing people associate with being recognized is feeling valued (88%), nearly 70% of people associated embarrassment or discomfort with the process of both giving and receiving [compliments]." (Littlefield, 2019)

What? How can that be? How can we marry the downside of compliments—embarrassment, discomfort, etc.—with the very natural craving to be appreciated? Some things just don't make sense. Fortunately, this is not a book on human physiology. But it *is* about workplace functionality and even more specifically about how we can better navigate the workplace, so we need to dig into the compliments conundrum a little deeper.

Knowing just how awkward most of us feel about compliments, I found myself motivated to understand exactly why. There's a lot of information on self-esteem, emotional maturity, setting expectations, humility and many other possible explanations. Ultimately, however, I landed right back on Littlefield's doorstep with what I think is a more complete explanation (and another great tidbit). He said, "What makes us uncomfortable is that compliments catch us by surprise."

Interesting! I'm seeing a pattern here. Now, if I piece together what we discussed in the first chapter regarding judgment *and* what Littlefield says about the negative experience of receiving surprise subjective feedback *and* our apparent discomfort about compliments, it makes more sense. It should no longer come as a surprise that *surprises* are in fact the problem. Think about it. I don't know about you, but I've experienced a few surprise parties in my life. Those are positive in theory, but when people threw them for me, not once was my style or hair on point, and I definitely recall having an "If only I had known!" feeling in my gut.

Perhaps the greatest value in World Compliment Day isn't that we intentionally recognize each other's finer points but that we are ready and willing to hear and share compliments knowing that that's the purpose of the day. Kind of like how on Valentine's Day we're not completely caught off guard by random professions of love from our colleagues and long-lost friends. In the context of compliments and World Compliment Day, I like to imagine channeling Oprah Winfrey during her "12 Days of Christmas" special and just handing out compliments like we hand out valentines on Valentine's Day: "Here's a compliment for you! And a compliment for you! And *you* get a compliment, and *you* get one, too!" The more compliments you give, the more you'll get and the less you'll be surprised when and why and while it's happening.

So let's celebrate World Compliment Day in a big way! Let's start there and then expand it. Make it normal. Make it a cards-and-confetti (and lollipops!) kind of day. Get yourself and your colleagues to the point where you're never surprised but are rather expectant. Not embarrassed, but confident. Be the example of someone who stands out by noticing others' good work and then complimenting that good work. And then watch as those same people begin to notice you and reciprocate. Disclaimer: you *actually* have to notice their work. Your compliments need to be genuine. Just sayin'… You already know that, though, because you are totally awesome, awesome, awesome.

This chapter covers compliments and standing out in your workplace for a reason. Not only are they mechanisms to get you moving up the leadership or compensation ladder—that's nice, of course, and moving up is a key objective for a lot of working people—but becoming comfortable with giving and receiving compliments will help you thrive. It isn't about getting to the top rung, it's about being in the workplace and surviving it like a national champion. You honestly deserve to feel good at work! You need to feel good at work for your own well-being. You may think that work is just a means to live your best life outside of work, but above all, you *need* to be happy physically and mentally in the workplace. Why? Because again, you are what you do.

Let's just start with the fact that the average person spends 90,000 hours at work during the span of their life. Ninety. *Thousand.* Hours. Spelling that out one word at a time feels really dramatic and insurmountable. Do you feel the weight of that number, too? Really, though, I'm going to park that big number there for anyone who is maybe *juuust* starting out on their career journey. Deep breaths. You've got this!

Not trying to brag or anything, but I just did the math and I'm at 61,440 hours. (Yes, I am accepting compliments about that.) But on a serious note, like 'em or not, you get compliments because you're doing good work. And because you're doing good work, you're standing out. So own it! Be the top of your pyramid with your fancy jazz hands, your big hair and bow (or not), doing your thing and showing your spirit and doing it all uniquely your way. You need to embrace the things that are great because—I'm just keepin' it real here—it's not always easy to stand out.

…Wait, what! What do I mean by that? Here I am giving you a pep talk about owning your awesomeness and then I tell you it's not that easy? What the heck! If you're like me, maybe you've spent some time in a profession where a lot of people have a similar job. I can relate to the fact that it's sometimes difficult to stand out when you're tasked with the same general responsibilities as the people around you and all of them are highly motivated and awesome in *their* own way. In such situations, you might find it difficult to get noticed. You might also be hesitant to deliberately outshine your peers, especially if you're socially connected to them outside of work. Don't be! Your hard work and positive attitude will inspire your colleagues and peers and will spark their competitive drive and all boats will rise. That doesn't mean you have to be the very best at your craft, the first to arrive every day or the one who raises their hand for every opportunity. It means you have to be *good*. Consistently good. You need to maximize your uniqueness, especially when you're in a crowded field. Eventually, you'll find your niche or it will find you and you'll stand out.

There was a time when I worked in a regional sales capacity, which meant there were about 20 other individuals who had exactly the same job description as I did. I really enjoyed that job—far more than I had expected I would, actually. A lovely example of a good surprise! And I was also fairly decent at the job. *But* I was new to it and had transferred into the division from the marketing side of the company. If you work in sales or marketing, you know that those two areas are populated by very different groups of people and there's often a bit of tension between them. Which is crazy seeing as the two are entirely symbiotic. (Of course, I only know that now upon reflection.) At any rate, there was either some skepticism about me taking on my new role or I had created that narrative in my mind. Regardless, I was both inspired to show everyone I could do it and nervous about appearing too audacious.

In cheerleading, this scenario is similar to when a person straight out of high school makes the collegiate competition team. People are watching, judging, making excuses for why someone younger or from outside the system might have more/different talent or trying to box them into being only their best abilities, like saying "They're a great stunter, but they can't tumble" or "She looks really strong and could be a good addition to the team, but she has no experience." It takes time and maturity to understand all of these reactions and respond thoughtfully.

One thing I've learned from reflecting on the time I spent watching new talent join the cheerleading team and being the person transitioning between corporate departments is this: don't be jelly, be driven! Look at the values you like in other people and adopt them. See what might be possible if you learn it for yourself and then go for it. Be the person who compliments talent with sincerity and then tucks a little motivation into their own pocket to hit a new high. It's simple, but difficult. It does help if you surround yourself with the right people who help fuel your progress and not your pride.

Lucky for me, in the corporate setting, I had an outstanding boss at the time of my transition from marketing to sales. Said boss eased me into the position with an incredible onboarding plan and allowed me to build upon my own unique talents. One of my greatest strengths turned out to be in data analysis and systems use. I love numbers, and they worked for me on the sales floor. I used them to organize my thoughts and speaking points and show my customers where they could make more of a profit and draw in consumers, and quite frankly, that success was celebrated. But you know what? I was less good—I'd say even "poor"—at taking in a whole marketplace and seeing the big picture. I think I still have work to do on that to this day. Fortunately, I love working on that skill.

However, in a classic plot twist, it turned out that my biggest internal sales competitor, a seasoned veteran in the division, was uh-MAZE-ing with the big picture and conversely not as strong with the data. He was the first to say, "Listen, I've got Southern California, Arizona and New Mexico. I need multicultural marketing and in-store supplies." He was a big-picture person, and I am still cheering for him to this day because he turned out to be my biggest supporter and I was his. I helped him with his data and customer-specific talking points, and he helped me understand the business for the West and the United States overall. He also helped me be a little more fun, for what it's worth. (Oh my gosh, those shots of Patrón!) But the big-picture man sure could rally! And he did. He understood the art of not taking things too seriously while still being a seriously good colleague and human. We shared; we cared; we collaborated; we encouraged each other. We maximized our own unique talents, and because we complimented each other's skills, our individual lights shone even more brightly. In the end, both of our markets improved. It was like metallic pom-poms: magical.

Again, everyone has their own style, and that's a good thing. We might subscribe to the same brand values or hold the same titles or be wearing the same uniforms, but we're all unique. Some people stand out because of their personality; some stand out for their ideas or their portfolio of accomplishments. Personally, I love the moment when you see a colleague shine in their own way and you think, "Wow! I didn't know they could do that!" I also always deeply admire and gravitate towards both the people who think in big-picture terms and the people who handle bad moments with the most grace. Those two skills aren't my best attributes, though I wish they were. They're just what stand out the most to me.

I share this because I think we can more easily recognize qualities and skills in others that we don't (yet) have ourselves or that we're still developing and then downplay our own strengths. That's all very natural—it's called the "social comparison process." In an article by Kendra Cherry titled "Social Comparison Theory in Psychology," the original social comparison theorist, psychologist Leon Festinger, "believed that we engage in this comparison process as a way of establishing a benchmark by which we can make accurate evaluations of ourselves." (VeryWellMind.com, 2022) I really like this original 1954 view of social comparison because it's positive and momentous and sounds more scientific than what we hear today, especially given the negative chatter that surrounds the effects of social media. Too often we hear about (or maybe even think and feel) the downside of social comparison, when jealousy and envy creep in. That's why I keep reminding you about your unique awesomeness and telling you to not be jelly, be driven!

As long as we maintain and use a positive lens as we travel through the workplace, we'll be looking and heading in the right direction both personally and professionally. The negative lens is what causes us to compare and subsequently despair. Don't use that lens! Obvi… The more you recognize and sincerely compliment the talents of others, the more your colleagues will return the favor. Soon you'll find out that just like Gemini, complimenting can be viewed from two perspectives: one external and one internal. Thinking about the act of complimenting externally, we need to quite literally compliment the strengths we see in each other with words of encouragement and celebration. Thinking internally, we need to compliment the strengths we see in others with our *own* strengths so that our whole workplace teams rise up and shine and *BOOM!* Shake, shake, shake the room! I know, that's a little cringey but I still love it and it perfectly compliments my thoughts on the matter.

MAKING THE
OTHER A-TEAM

"You just have to stay positive,
no matter what happens."

STEVE KIRKLAND, KANSAS STATE UNIVERSITY

t's important to hold on to that feeling of standing out and all of
the positive emotions and forward momentum that comes with
it, because this chapter isn't so…shall we say?…peppy. I've mentioned that I've always noticed people who handle bad moments with
the most grace. I've also mentioned that those people are not always
me. I'm improving, but it's been a journey, not a teleport. Still, like
so many other themes in this book, my objective is to give you a leg
up in your workplace journey so that you start out ahead of where I
did. Or at least so that you know you aren't alone when you experience some of the same things.

Before you get to the good part of life where you're standing out
like the shining star you are, there's the hard, exhausting, sometimes

deflating part of life when you're learning and honing your craft. Often, despite your very best efforts, there's someone better than you. The truth is, there will *always* be someone better. Gah! I know, that doesn't feel good to hear. Believe me, it doesn't feel good to say, either, but it's something I've learned over time. And actually, it only makes me raise my own bar higher, so that's alright. It's okay. It really is, because we're gonna do this anyway!

Not only can you lead by example, you can *follow* by example. In cheerleading, as you learn new chants, cheers and routines, you're always standing behind the choreographer or the captain—basically, people who already know the drill. They show you the moves in smaller bits, going one at a time until you're ready to put them all together. So you're following, but you're also learning to do it on your own. You not only learn step-by-step how to build that pyramid, that system, that business plan, you learn how to build your confidence.

In the workplace, if you're able to recognize and appreciate another person for their strength or leadership or creativity or smarts or whatever other moves and qualities make them shine brightly in your eyes, consider such recognition as a type of roadmap that will guide you to the next level of success. Remember, *this* type of social comparison—the admiration and the benchmarking—leads to focusing and preparing for how *you* want to be in the workplace. Learn from watching and then try to implement those qualities in a way that's uniquely yours.

Imitation really is flattery, and leaders like knowing that a new team member is teachable. So ask questions and show interest and pay attention, because despite knowing that you aren't the be-all and end-all of everything in your office from Day One, you also know that you're going to commit yourself to being your very best and that you're already pretty fabulous anyway. And when the time is right and when you've shown yourself to be up to the task, the windows of opportunity will open. They really will. However, they don't always open when you expect they will or should. You might try for a new opportunity, put your name in the hat, sit for an interview… and not make the cut. It stinks. It happens. So then what? What happens when those windows *don't* open? What happens when you fail to make the cut and get the opportunity you're going for?

What happens is that you try your darndest to handle those harder moments with grace even though it might be incredibly difficult. But you go for grace because people like me and you and your peers and your current and future workplace advocates are watching.

In a moment, I'll provide a more specific best-practice tactic to employ when you've lost out on an opportunity, namely doing so with grace as well as hindsight (also known as metacognition mixed with a side of humility), but first, I want to take some lines on the page to recognize the very real experience of depression that can set in while job-seeking. It can even set in as you're slogging through a workplace role that you're not enjoying or are ready to move on from. They don't call it the "daily grind" for nothing!

I'm sharing this because whether it's you or a friend or a colleague of yours, you should at the very least be aware of the fact that according to Mental Health America (https://www.mhanational.org/depression-workplace), "depression tends to affect people in their prime working years." If you're reading this book, that's probably you. That's us. Further, the Society for Human Resource Management (SHRM) acknowledged that nearly a quarter (23%) of workers surveyed "reported that they had been diagnosed with depression at some point in their lifetime, and approximately 40% of *those* survey participants said that they had taken time off work to deal with their condition." That 23% is a big number with big consequences! There's an extreme likelihood that you know those people or are one of them yourself.

The good news is that the vast majority of people push or pull through their experience with depression, but like so many other things in life, it takes a village. Be a part of that village. Educate yourself about depression and then do your best to be a good listener, an encourager and an includer. These are important workplace qualities no matter what the situation is, but they are critical qualities when supporting a colleague or any peer who's experiencing depression. I missed the signs of depression in the lives of my friends and colleagues at least twice that I'm (now) aware of, possibly even more. I was young, opinionated and yet uneducated on the topic; I was full of serotonin, dopamine, oxytocin and endorphins. In short, I was a lot to take. But now, having fumbled a time or two and learned from it, I take every opportunity to address the seriousness of the subject whenever I can. As I said at the start of this chapter, my goal is to give you a head start or a jump start in your own workplace, depending on where you are along your path. Depression stops people in their tracks, it's true, but I believe we are hardwired with a primal need to move forward and grow.

There's an often-used saying in business that if you're not growing, you're dying. That's brash and I want so badly to disagree with it, but I think the saying is at least mostly true. Although I most often hear it in reference to an organization as a whole, it rings true for individuals as well. Sure, we can simply sustain ourselves for a short while, but ultimately, we're all getting older, so why not *grow* older?

Sustaining ourselves in the workplace does provide balance and survival—it's like a sort of professional homeostasis—but simply sustaining means we miss out on the opportunity to thrive.

In contrast, *growing* is more intentional and deliberate. It means putting yourself out there by daring to try new things, learn new information, gain skills and go for opportunities. If you do that, you'll move forward and grow even though you might not always realize you're growing in the moment, especially when that aforementioned window doesn't open. But you *are* still growing! I can prove it with my own personal examples. Sometimes the examples and anecdotes I share are the big, exciting wins I've experienced (frankly, it's quite enjoyable to share them), but in this chapter, in this moment, it feels much more poignant to share my very real failures to better articulate my point. Ah, if only there weren't so many to choose from!

To validate that you aren't alone (or to comfort you when you experience a letdown), let me share three personal experiences I've had with rejection. The first experience was way, way back in junior high school, when I qualified for an advanced math placement in the following year. Sadly (but also with a twinge of humor), this surprised everyone except me—*I* knew I loved math—because I was lagging in other subject areas. Seeing as I was the lone voice of excitement amidst a sea of skeptical adults, the decision was made to keep me in a lower math level for a subsequent year. Not surprisingly to me, I continued to do well in math. Ultimately, I was also inspired to improve my performance in other classes in order to validate my abilities to the naysayers. Well, I'm happy to say that after two more years, I actually made and joined the high school math relay team, one of my proudest accomplishments to this day. That was likely when I first gained a sense of agency, in owning my own journey. (However, I'm still a little annoyed with myself for miscalculating that *one* question about how many days it would take the slug to climb up the wall if he slid back down a little each night. Rookie mistake! I forgot that once the little bugger got to the top of the well, he'd be out, which meant I didn't have to calculate that he slid back down that night. It happens. Whatevs… Clearly, I'm over it. Or not.)

In another example of success over failure, about eight years later, as I was wrapping up my undergraduate studies, I literally mailed letters to a *hundred* zoos and aquariums in the United States in the hopes of obtaining a position within a communications department. I know for certain it was a hundred because I recall thinking that it was a nice round number and it felt very intentional. The fruits of that labor were responses from only two organizations, both of which offered an unpaid internship. After shedding a few tears over the lack of opportunity and the unrequited cost of a dream, postage and fancy résumé paper (100% cotton in ivory; not quite Elle Woods material, but I was nonetheless proud of the effort), I learned that while letters are nice, personal connections go a *lot* further. I needed to know people or at least people who knew people in the right places.

Today, personal connections are more important to me than anything in the workplace, although anyone who knows me on a social level will tell you that I still love good quality paper and actual letters (just not form letters). Additionally, that letter-writing and letter-failing experience instilled an internal desire to be a connector to people around me who are chasing their own dreams. There's nothing more fulfilling to me now than helping point people in their right direction! That's my pre-plug for mentorship, but I'll write more about that later. Stay tuned…

The third big failure I'll share occurred roughly ten years after the résumés-to-zoos experience, when I was attending the third interview for my dream job. It was probably the dream job for a million people! No exaggeration, it was at one of the world's biggest, bada$$iest consumer products companies, and I was the *only* remaining candidate for the position. In other words, it was between me and not me. And guess what? I bombed. I bombed real good. A solid game-over event. I thought that because the company had come after me for an opportunity, I was a shoo-in. I literally wasted two hours of the interviewer's time talking about myself and all of my accomplishments without connecting any of that whatsoever to the company's organizational needs. The company was a different industry than the one I was working in at the time, and I hadn't done any research on their consumers, their competition, their challenges or their needs.

Unlike where I'd been at the time of my junior high letdown, I had the total skill set this company needed. Unlike how I'd been in my early 20s (when I was chasing dreams of holding up baby golden lion tamarins, pink fairy armadillos and red pandas with Jack Hanna on *The Late Show with David Letterman*), I had personal connections to the organization and the person who was interviewing me. Unlike those two earlier experiences, *this* time the growth I had not yet achieved was humility.

That episode is horrifying to look back on, but I assure you, I haven't made the same mistake since. What I learned the most from that rejection is that relationships within the context of jobs and the workplace are no different than everyday human relationships. It's imperative to stay tuned to what the other person/entity needs in order for the relationship to become and remain healthy. It's a give-give relationship, not a give-take one. For what it's worth, I'll add that not only did I learn my lesson, I *so* completely learned my lesson that in other interviews since the very-not-humble one, I've actually overwhelmed the interviewer and didn't get the job then, either. Alas, there is a happy medium. You need to find it for yourself. Consider it a badge of honor when you get it just right!

All of these examples are to say that my advice on the best-practice tactic to employ when you lose out on an opportunity is to reflect on your own situation and actions. Do you need more skill or experience? Do you need to develop deeper personal connections and a broader network? Do you know what the company is looking for in a candidate and is the company's culture the right fit for you and you for it?

Don't just reflect on the exact experience of the interview, also consider the lead-up to the interview *and* the post-interview experience. Don't blow that second opportunity, either, for Pete's sake! Take that post-interview, post-letdown moment with grace and reflect on it. You'll grow without even knowing you're growing. And don't just reflect in the moment, reflect over time. If you've read Dan Sullivan's book *The Gap and The Gain*, you know that measuring backwards from where you are to where you started is critical. Thinking about where I am now versus where I was then, I can certainly see that all of my major failures only set me up for growth.

If my experiences aren't speaking to you, you'll find more related content in the Losing Slumps & Winning Streaks chapter, where I share more well-known examples of people who have picked themselves up and moved forward with great success. What's important to realize from these examples is that no matter who you are, letdowns happen…but also no matter who you are, you have what it takes to get up and go, fight, win!

PRACTICE

TOSS-TO-HANDS

"Every once in a while, life throws you an opportunity. Stepping up when those opportunities come along is crucial for career growth, but it can be intimidating. Have confidence in your abilities, be courageous and go all-in."

WINDLE JARVIS, GEORGE MASON UNIVERSITY

You did it! You've arrived! Where you are today means you made the cut, got the job (whew!) and joined the team. Congratulations! Now, exactly how did you do that and what do you do next?

In cheerleading, one of the foundational moves you learn is a stunt called a shoulder stand. You know what that is even if you weren't a cheerleader—it's the same shoulder stand you learned in a pool, in a shallow lake or on a beach starting way back as early as you could swim. If you didn't have a favorite water spot, maybe you learned the shoulder stand in your friend's backyard when you'd just lost your ball over the fence. Probably learning it involved being slippery with water or sweat and the person holding you on their shoulders being wobbly. *You* were probably wobbly. Perhaps somebody was trying to push you off, thinking that was funny. Maybe you were freaking out and were slightly afraid of your new height in the world. Regardless, it was hard. In cheerleading, it's ever so slightly easier to move upward and reach a new height, primarily because cheerleaders have a few options for arriving on top of someone's shoulders from dry land. It's kind of similar to how we arrive at our jobs.

The first route up to shoulder level isn't necessarily the easiest way up, it's just the way that most people initially make progress. It's the slow, safe way. You begin by holding on to another person's hands and stepping onto their leg with one foot, right in the crease where their leg turns into their hip. Then you put your other foot on their opposite shoulder. Then you lift that first foot to the available shoulder. Eventually, you're standing on both of their shoulders and steadying yourself, still holding their hands. Then you carefully straighten yourself up into a standing position.

Oh, and by the way, you started off behind them while they were semi squatting down. They couldn't see you at all—the most they could do to help you on your way up was to stay still and have strong arms and wait until you're ready before *they* fully stand up. It takes a while to get into the right position for a shoulder stand, but when you arrive there, it's usually nice and sturdy because you were very deliberate about where you planted your feet and how long you held on before you were ready to let go. Even your partner was very deliberate about their role in getting you to the next level—every little step was planned out. That's no different than climbing the proverbial career ladder.

Sometimes I feel as if that was the path I took throughout most of my early workplace experience. It was certainly the long, hard, slow route I took to my first career-type job out of college. I never had any significant college or career counseling outside of various personality tests—I simply perused junk mail and "Help Wanted" signs that were posted on bulletin boards with pushpins. Ah, the pre-internet days… Recall those hundred letters I sent out? I had populated those with names and addresses I found in a (very likely outdated) printed industry manual from the Association of Zoos and Aquariums.

Note that I landed in a totally different industry after all of that work. Slow route. However, very true to cheer metaphor form, when I did finally land my first career job, I was on sturdy ground, in part because it was the first respectable employment I was offered. Also, I really needed the income. It was good for me and good for my employer. I could have stayed there for years and years if I wanted, because—quite frankly—the company was desperate to keep people in that position. While it did offer standard benefits, it paid poorly and it was relatively unstimulating, at least for me. That said, it wasn't a total mismatch with my interests—I absolutely loved the product, brand and company. In fact, I still do! It's just that the specific *nature* of the job wasn't ultimately for me. Also, what I know now is that when companies are desperate to fill positions that are chronically difficult to fill, they're not likely to quickly promote anyone *out* of those positions no matter how skilled they are. Lesson learned! After less than two years, I knew I needed to try climbing again, because the harder I worked to improve in that job space, the more I was cementing my future *in that job space*. So, the second climb commenced! But this time, the career "path" was a tiny bit easier to tread. I'll revert to a cheer metaphor again to explain why.

The second way up to a higher level in cheerleading is called the walk-up. You begin by facing the wrong direction and stepping into someone's hands and trusting that they'll help lift you to the next level whilst you complete a half-twist of your body during the upward transition. Believe it or not, this is actually a little easier than the climb-up-the-person's-back way and definitely faster. *But* this second way usually entails a few initial misfires, a little more training, and a lot more trust, which early on can be unnerving.

That second way was how I arrived at my second significant workplace experience. In that case, I had a connection to a recruiter and I went into the job interview with a little more confidence even though I couldn't see exactly where I would end up. It was just listed as "an open position" in marketing at "company confidential". It turned out it was a pretty cool company. I was offered the job and I took it. For me, it was a career *change*, not a career move. I had no long-term plan—I just had a need for something else, something that offered more intellectual stimulation and better financial security.

Ultimately, my new job was a level up from the previous one. Actually, let's be honest and say that it was a half-level up, but that sort of kills the metaphor, so just ignore that fact. The new job paid a little better and I was a little more challenged and liked the nature of what I was doing on a day-to-day basis a little more. Since we're talking about little things, I'll take a little editorial side trip here to share that one of the things I've learned along my career journey is that we need to experience personal growth to secure our well-being. Remember, if you're not growing, you're dying! (I still don't like the way that sounds, but again, it's still mostly true.) Psychologists widely agree with this general sentiment and say in order to grow, three psychological needs need to be met: competence, relatedness and autonomy. (Shahram, 2019)

In this new, a-little-bit-better workplace, I achieved competence, but there was little relatedness and no autonomy. The job had all the potential to be great fun except that I was the single staff member of two departments: group sales and public relations. Out of perhaps ten full-time staff, I had *two* layers of management watching and dictating my every move. I lasted three years there before the fact that two-thirds of my psychological needs were not being met started rattling around in my brain and urged me on to another change. Still trying to wrap my arms around the geopolitical spectrum of the workplace, I did another metaphorical walk-up. This time, however, the person lifting me up was taller and the view began to change.

By some degree of luck, my third workplace landing led to an exciting, challenging, fulfilling 15-year career, during which time I became more fully aware of the fundamental difference between a career *change* and a career *move*. That workplace was also where I came to understand and exploit the values of being well-rounded, focusing on personal touches and networking. It was where I improved my competencies and gained relatedness and autonomy. Even better, it was where all of those values aligned and I got my first ever toss-to-hands.

The toss-to-hands in cheerleading is the third traditional path to getting to a shoulder stand and also the fastest path to reaching the next level. It is quite literally the act of somebody holding you by the waist and strategically throwing you up into the air and then catching your feet. All you have to do is jump up and stay straight unless you are Gabi Butler and all kinds of extra! If you aren't Gabi Butler, than with this method, the other person does almost all of the work based on the assumption that you won't noodle out and make them look bad in the process.

I've been metaphorically tossed-to-hands twice during the entire span of my workplace career, and both times were monumental occasions that changed my life. I will be forever grateful to everyone involved. They changed the secondary choices I made, the way I planned and strategized inside *and* outside of the workplace, the way my colleagues viewed me as a professional and (sad to say, but true) the way I viewed myself. I highly recommend this method of moving up. It's fast and it's fulfilling. It feels amazing. And when and if you've gained the skills and/or confidence you need and you're ready for the window or door to open, you will fly up and soar! I told you this day would arrive!

Very specifically, these toss-to-hands career opportunities hadn't been posted—they were jobs that key individuals asked me to take and were highly desirable positions and multi-rung leaps up the career ladder. More generally, these were the kinds of jobs that make skeptics say, "How did *you* get that job?" Meanwhile, the people who know you best say, "You are *perfect* for that job!" These were the kinds of jobs that people who envy you feel they were snubbed from but that give hope to and fuel confidence in the people who admire you, the people who are hanging out with you over on the positive side of the social comparison theory.

The workplace toss-to-hands happens when you have consistently put your best foot forward and you have spread your wings in anticipation of what could come next, ready to catch that breeze. But the critical piece is that you must never stop anticipating that gust of good wind! You can never rest on your laurels; you must always show appreciation for the people who lift you up. You need to keep growing every day and return that favor whenever and wherever possible.

So go on and soar, why don't you! And while you're up there, lift up others. Be the person who holds, lifts or tosses others into a better space. Even though it doesn't always feel like this will be the case, I promise that all good deeds *do* come back around. Remember that sometimes you have to make changes before you can really move. Sometimes you have to follow those who can't see you; sometimes the way up has twists and turns. Sometimes the best way up is out and the best way forward is sideways. No matter what, though, you can't go anywhere in *any* direction unless you make a move.

Most of all, realize that you are always and forever simultaneously the person doing the holding *and* the person doing the climbing. Be the person who has a sturdy foundation, broad shoulders and nimble hands and also be the person who infuses honest-to-goodness sweat equity, trust and pep (for good measure) into the workplace while you're on your way up.

OFFENSE, DEFENSE AND EVERYTHING ELSE

"I think it's important to immerse yourself. I always prided myself on being a utility player...having the ability to perform in any position needed. My advice is to learn all aspects of the job so you have a complete knowledge base of every position to set you up for success when moving up the ladder."

MIKE O'HALLORAN, CENTRAL MICHIGAN UNIVERSITY

n collegiate cheerleading, you don't just need to know how to cheer (which is complex enough), you need to know the game. And not just one game, you need to know literally all of them. *All* of the games and *all* of the sports—the rules, the records, the terminology, the seasonality. You also need to know who the players and coaches are, of your team and of theirs. You need to know the VIPs who funded the field or the court or the arena and who have courtside or box season tickets. You need to know the folks in the athletic department and all of the super fans who lead various alumni groups. You need to know this, because despite the hard work you've done to hone your own craft and get to the level you're at, you're no longer playing a club sport. The competition and fans are no longer there just to watch you, and you are no longer relegated to simply playing a position. You're playing a *role*, and that role is ambassador. Progressing through the workplace is no different.

Whether it's through college, trade school, or on-the-job training, you start by honing your technical craft. During this time, you're observed and tested on your individual skills and knowledge. Then you move from mastering a skill to mastering a set of skills to mastering a subject matter. At this stage, you're likely beginning to apply your knowledge—perhaps you're working in groups or within a chain of command. You're likely experiencing feedback not only on your skills, but also your talents. Have you completed your tasks *and* do you work well with others? Do you follow directions clearly *and* with confidence? Can you successfully resolve issues *and* leave the workplace in good order?

In order to continue moving upward through or to an organization, you'll need to know a lot more than what's in your subject matter, a.k.a. your job description. You need to be better than book smart or street smart. As you move up in the workplace over time, your scope of responsibility and influence will grow whether you like it or not. It's called "experience," and even though your individual skills are tremendously important—it's not likely you'd be where you are today without them—*how* you infuse those skills into the way you work with others is what becomes ever more important even as you continue to gain more experience.

The way you involve yourself in the business of growing and starting waves—not in the bleachers, but in your department, the greater organization, or an entire industry—starts to matter, at least unless you intend to curtail your career. (In fact, the more experience you gain in the workplace, the more people will ask "What have you done?" rather than "Where have you worked?") This is especially true of small organizations, where it might be easy to think you've reached the pinnacle of your trade because you have nobody visible ahead of you who's doing it better, nor do you have anyone behind you who's chasing their own career dreams and subsequently you. But this principle also pertains to larger organizations, where statements like "Works well with others," "Worked cross functionally," "Opened up lines of communication" and "Created a joint task force" start to populate annual reviews.

At this stage of your career development, the offense and defense of an organization are muddled—they're made up of marketing and sales collaboration teams, research and supply chain experts, human resources and IT professionals and many others. Your colleagues are the athletes and the coaches. And you? *You* are an ambassador. You need the broadest possible perspective to get and keep a competitive advantage.

When I did a walk-up to my third career change, I landed at an organization that—to this day!—is unparalleled in both brand recognition and brand affinity. Honestly, the statistical chances that I would have ever noticed the posted job opportunity I landed have got to be incredibly, incredibly low. Suffice to say that to this day, I thank Monster.com! It's old-school now, but way back in the year 2000, the Monster.com algorithms said, "Hey! You might like this job!" and I was like, "Wow! You're totally right!" Monster.com was way before LinkedIn, but the concept is similar, and it worked a miracle for me. Although it wasn't a zoo or an aquarium or my childhood dream job, the position did marry several of my biggest areas of interest with my education and experience *and* it was within the communications department of one of the top companies and brands in the world.

How I came to have that job is humbling to reflect on now. It also definitely makes me nervously laugh a little to think of how close I came to missing out on that job or other opportunities I never would have even noticed or taken a chance on because I wasn't looking. I went into the interview process and subsequently the position with a lot of unsubstantiated confidence, certainly much more than I should have had as far as the technical aspects of the role were concerned. I remember thinking that I literally had all of the work experience the job posting asked for, so therefore, I must be a good fit. And thank goodness for an over-inflated ego, because while I did indeed have the work experience, I wouldn't say I was especially gifted at my trade. On top of that, I was entering the kind of competitive work environment I'd never experienced before. However, when the hiring agent asked me what some of my major accomplishments were (the "What have you done?" question), I was able to say that I had moved myself across the country to chase opportunities, worked two full-time jobs, obtained my master's degree and completed a marathon in my spare time. She thought that was a story with a good hook even though I had failed the press release formatting quiz. I had something she thought she could work with. I was some*one* she thought she could work with. I got the job. Hoorah!

Every senior leader at this company not only worked well beyond their job description, they had done something big and meaningful along their career journey. Some had worked for other top-tier global consumer brands; others had honest-to-goodness worked their way up entirely through this one company over decades. As far as I could see, *those* individuals were the savviest of all—they had survived lay-offs, reorganizations, new leadership, department consolidation, consultants, talent searches, globalization and more. Suddenly, my four years of relevant experience and my willingness to travel 50% of the time seemed totally insignificant and insufficient compared with the performance requirements that lay ahead of me.

My new job called for a great deal of writing, which I thoroughly enjoyed. However, it wasn't a craft I'd fully honed. I also hadn't learned to navigate a huge corporate structure or rein in my excessively bubbly personality, which I realize is often misinterpreted as immaturity or even insincerity. But one of the first responsibilities I had was to give tours of our manufacturing facility to special guests, and through giving those tours, I met people from other departments and at different hierarchical levels within the organization. I also wrote the company newsletter and found exciting people and stories coming out of all corners of the campus. (When you're looking for good and interesting tidbits, you always find them!) I helped decide on and fulfill grant requests and I got to know the company's local community and its leaders. I was one of a handful of spokespersons for the company and traveled throughout the United States and Canada promoting our products, our brand and our purpose.

At the intersection of all of these to-do's, I gained a broader perspective of my role and the part it played within the whole organization. Slowly but surely, I was learning more than just my job tasks—I was learning about the company, the culture, the consumer, the customer and the industry. I was definitely morphing into an ambassador!

Fortunately, time, perseverance and red-pen editing from my immediate boss afforded me the opportunity to improve the technical skills required for my job description while I simultaneously gained the experience I needed to start making waves. With experience, I was able to stretch beyond my job description and use my genuine interest in other people and my team mentality to do things beyond what was expected of me: I organized external runs and internal rallies, facilitated foreign-language classes, infused more humor and fun into annual meetings and wrote and filmed submission scripts for our human resources director's reality television show application. I didn't know it then—I was entirely naïve—but the combination of my basic job responsibility (to know something about all aspects of our business) and my willingness to jump in and say "yes" no matter what definitely got me to where I went throughout that organization. It also got me to where I am today. I remain a loyal ambassador for the brand even though I'm no longer there.

I'm confident that gaining a broader perspective of the organization fueled me taking personal responsibility for my growth even though the position I was in hadn't changed drastically since I first began. The job hadn't changed, *I* had. Within just a couple of years, my specialty of connecting people and my knack of encouraging teamwork and pep ultimately gelled, and I found myself in a position of saying "yes" to someone else's request for help at just the right moment, namely when that person was empowered to let me run with an idea and trusted me enough to believe that I would succeed.

At the time, one of our company's key account managers wanted to do something special for an important retail customer and was looking for help. He didn't know exactly what he wanted to do, so he ventured through the office building to the marketing and public relations wing. Just like the Monster.com algorithms had worked for me, he found me in that PR wing, ready with a suggestion and an open mind. He asked if I wanted to help him think of something effective and sincere, and I said, "YES!"

With his supportive go-ahead and accompanied by a wave of individuals who raised their hands to help out (basically all of the fun people), we convinced hundreds of colleagues to dress in red and clap enthusiastically while standing around a red carpet, a statue of a dog and an external team of buyers we wanted to woo. And woo we did! We showed the buyers just how important their relationship was to our company, and I showed the key account manager just how much I valued his trust in me. That small moment of success—really maybe an hour in total—quickly led me to a new and exciting opportunity in a different department, where I filled in during a colleague's short-term maternity leave. After she returned from leave, I wound up in yet another new and exciting role, this time a much-coveted, long-term maternity leave relief position in Australia. The person who gave me that Australia opportunity was the same key account manager who'd thrown a request and an opportunity my way a year earlier. That second opportunity was the result of being open and able; it was my first ever toss-to-hands.

The red-carpet, clapping-colleagues, dog-statue, "yes" event wasn't my first-ever workplace success story. Some of the others were even bigger successes if you count the total number of impressions they made or how well they've been remembered over time. But upon reflection, I do think the red-carpet event was the turning point for when I began having steady and dependable forward momentum at work. It was when the wins began to outnumber the losses and ties and when the times I didn't make the cut or was appointed as an alternate decreased and the times I made the team increased. That was when I intentionally started seeking out opportunities that maximized my strengths and included more people who believed in and trusted me and led me to bigger plays. I began to more fully understand the long game and how to better align myself with incredible coaches and mentors and other inspiring colleagues at every level of business. *That* was when I became my own ambassador.

The Center for Creative Leadership says that a broader perspective is a must-have for career advancement. I will attest to that truth! I will also say that in order to have a broader perspective, you need to have the willingness to learn and the ability to learn…and you need to know *how* you learn. In my experience, I've realized it's easier to find the *ability* to learn when you are placed in a completely new environment and there's a sense of "it's okay not to know" for both the learner and the learner's surrounding team. Conversely, it's generally harder to learn if you are competing against your pride when the expectation is that you already have what it takes to do the job. That said, though, it took some time for me to learn *how* I learned best.

It turns out that I'm a jump-in kind of person. I need full immersion. I can see now how that need can be its own kind of roadblock. For me and many others like me, to be fully immersed in an opportunity means that somebody else has to throw us the ball. Somebody else has to be confident and competent enough with their own abilities and interests to momentarily set them aside and let us take the shot. This reality validates the case for giving it all you've got even when you're "just" practicing, even when you think nobody is watching…because the people who *are* watching don't have all the time in the world to constantly set their balls down and cheer for you as you make your way towards the goal. Those moments are gold! And they present themselves at random intervals no matter where you are along your workplace continuum. That's why you should always assume that someone is scouting for just *your* talents. Someone is looking for more than a set of skills or a body to fill a position—they're looking for someone who can catch the ball and carry it forward. They're looking for an ambassador, a real all-around team player.

Somebody somewhere right now is handling too many balls of their own, and they're looking to make a pass. They're watching the way you work, the way you treat others, the way you listen, the way you speak up and the way you raise your hand to say, "Yes! Pick me!" Somebody is noticing your hard work and talents, and you *will* be rewarded. It might take a little time—in my case, it took eight years—and it will definitely require persistence, but that ball *will* be passed your way. Are you ready?

TEAM CAPTAINS

*"A leader, wherever they are in an organization,
is a person who is perceptive, who can bring
people together, who can kind of distill all of
the great ideas into a thing that works."*

WHEI WONG, UNIVERSITY OF NORTH CAROLINA AT CHAPEL HILL

There's a lot of pressure on the top layers of leadership in the business world to have tremendous experience, tenure and staying power. To be the penultimate ambassadors of the company and give half-time-worthy speeches with every internal or external interaction. "The market crashed? We will weather this storm! Global supply chain disruption? We will pave a new way forward! Total organizational restructuring and new pillars of success? Let's rebuild this plane in midair!"

I've been the beneficiary of some of those speeches, actually. I've specifically and literally benefited from each and every one of those speeches (and maybe helped write parts of them, too). Each one provided me with a little surge of workplace adrenaline, focus and determination.

For sure, my workplace internal flame got legit lit, but I don't think it's healthy to depend on those kinds of speeches for your everyday motivation. I'm not suggesting that passion and conviction and great vocal deliverance won't add to a leader's effectiveness or a follower's focus, I'm just saying that it's a little unfair and a lot of a cop-out to think that somebody *else* needs to be the end-all, be-all of every conversation, decision and strategy. Folks, we need to lean in and be a *part* of the process, not just a beneficiary! We need to be the hype guy just as much as anyone else we might look up to. We've got this!

The idea that every speck of responsibility to motivate you should fall on one set of shoulders (or the leadership team's collective shoulders) and that you exist entirely to fulfill the will of leadership's decisions is so late, it's not even 2008. Seriously! First, that attitude implies that you aren't able to motivate yourself, which is clearly inaccurate seeing as you're currently reading a book that has the word "cheerleader" in the title. Second, I listened to those talks in an employee cafeteria or in the foyer of an office building, standing on the stairs with the hushing buzz of white noise suffusing the background as my colleagues stood around wondering just how great or grim the news was going to be. Honestly, I think those talks are mostly effective because the expectations are often so low to begin with—everyone thinks they're about to lose their job, so anything other than that is bound to make them jubilant. (Sidenote on the whiteboard to all current and future leaders, which is to say all of you: meet with your team often and often meet your team with good news.)

What we should all realize is that all of those big town hall speeches begin with "we"! Take to heart that nothing can be accomplished without everyone's collective yet individual contribution. When you consider it that way, what becomes glaringly obvious is that we shouldn't look to our leaders to be siloed decision-makers. In fact, leaders should mostly be fans, and not just fans of the company or the industry! They need to mostly be fans of *us*. They should be our biggest fans and our biggest cheerleaders.

I once had a manager who—during a disappointing but quite accurate annual review of my performance—said, "You're really great at identifying the problems and potential roadblocks. What I'd like you to also be is really great at identifying the solutions." That stuck with me. Oh, it stuck real good! Clearly—I'm writing about it now, roughly 20 years later. The manager's feedback actually was constructive, and I reflect on it constantly in a vast number of applications: my work, my health, my interpersonal skills, my parenting tactics, you name it. I think about it so often that I sometimes wonder what would have materialized in my workplace journey had I not received that specific feedback. That same manager could have simply counseled and judged me on the minutiae of my work, like how I crafted a press release, how well I worked with others, my organizational skills, etc. But instead, he counseled me on the big picture. *My* personal big picture. He didn't just help me become a better worker or a better colleague, he helped me become a better person. *That* is what a leader should do. That's what fans do! They shout, "L.E.T.S.G.O.— Let's go!" That's plural. That's the nosotros form in Spanish. They're there *with you*. They're there. What a fun sentence is that? And not in the condescending way, as in "There, there." Big difference. Huge. It's all about the semantics...

In cheerleading, the leader of the team doesn't look any different from everyone else, but they *make* a big difference. They might be a little more senior (or an actual senior) or more experienced than most of the team, but they don't wear a special badge or necessarily stand at the top of the pyramid. The captain is in the thick of it, just like everyone else. The difference in what they know compared with what less-experienced individuals know (who are focusing on their own rise) is that if all of the individuals on the team are at the top of their own game, then the whole structure will have more stability. The better the person standing next to you becomes, the better you want to become. The stronger your partner is, the stronger you want to be.

Team captains are effective because they lead from within, from underneath, from behind and from in front. In a 2018 TEDx presentation, executive leadership coach Lolly Daskal said, "We think leadership is an external quality, but it is and always has been an internal quality. Leaders aren't always great because they have power, but because they can empower others."

In cheerleading and in so many corners of civic life (including boardrooms and most elected positions), the leaders of an organization are rotated; they usually have strict term limits and there are usually some parameters around who's considered to be qualified. For example, cheerleading captains generally have to be a junior or a senior to qualify for the role. It's likely that juniors and seniors have at least a couple of years of experience under their pom-poms, although there's no expectation that they should be the technical best at the sport of cheerleading. They aren't put in the position of captain to show off their phenomenal rallying skills or their perfect bucket fists or to make every decision. Rather, they're made captains to ensure that the collective whole moves in the right direction at the right time. The captain looks at the squad in tandem with the coach and uses their insider's eye to help figure out who would make great partners, how much more practice is needed in order to achieve individual and team goals and which events are must-dos and which are a drain on the team's capacity. The captain is the person who says "You look tired—why don't you sit this one out?" or "I heard you had a great idea! Why don't you bring it up at the meeting?" A lot of times people say that a leader should be a big-picture thinker. While there's value to that, I believe that the leader who minds the pennies is the leader who sees the dollars come rolling in. (Apparently, so does Benjamin Franklin, who allegedly "coined" that phrase. Couldn't resist…)

Now, if you're keeping track, you'll realize that in the last chapter I told you that while you work your way up the workplace ladder, you need to think beyond your own duties to fully appreciate the scope and scale of why you're employed at all. Then in this chapter, I told you that as a leader, you often need to think smaller. It's a conundrum. If it came from the mouth of Yoda, it would probably sound more like, "Truly small the big thoughts of a leader are." Neither my version of the point nor Yoda's is perfectly stated, but both are perfectly clear. If the answer is that you must first advocate for yourself by thinking big and then prove yourself through the little things, the question then becomes, at what point do you make the transition from thinking big to thinking small? My response to this will expose why I'm generally an advocate for term limits and job rotation in a variety of applications, but especially in the workplace.

If you can, stop yourself from reading for a moment and instead pause to think of your mind and your personal development as an estuary, with all of the small but vital waterways branching off and meandering to and fro throughout the lowlands just before earth turns to sea and sea turns to earth. (Cue the spa music and light breeze effect while we pause to let you stop reading…) Maybe there's a batch of cattails over to the left and a great blue heron to the right, both plant and animal soaking up the water and sunlight. In these brackish waters, high tides bring in vital oxygen and nutrients while transporting out sediments and waste; the low tides offer a chance for land creatures to rest, hydrate, build shelters and repopulate. This in-and-out nature of the water flow and salinity levels provides for some of the most productive ecosystems in the world.

We should aim to be just like that in our personal endeavors! Really, why not? Tell me that last paragraph didn't feel calm and relaxing. (I almost fell asleep writing it...) But seriously, following the rhythms of nature is, well, natural. The folks over at Peeler Associates, experts in helping leaders grow, are pickin' up what I'm puttin' down, too. They say, "Some of a leader's best thinking and learning occurs in that space in between when all is still. It's known as the 'creative pause,' a term probably coined by the best-selling author Edward de Bono, and it refers to the increasingly rare downtime that leaders have to rest and to quietly reflect."

It's exactly because this space in between is *so* beneficial to our brain that I think the space in between is also beneficial to an organization. If you can wrap your mind around a Mr. Miyagi mindset of "Wax on, wax off" in the workplace, you might consider what would happen if you yourself endorsed such a process of rotating leadership in the workplace. In a world where tenure rules and it feels like you need to protect all power and assets once you accumulate them lest they leave you, realize that you might just be doing yourself and your organization a disservice to linger. If your organization isn't set up in such a way that rotating is easy or possible, at least be sure to steward new ideas, new inspirations, new examples and new interests so that your perspectives can continue to grow.

In the cheerleading world, once a captain relinquishes their title, they take their leadership skills and apply them to a new endeavor, one where they create another mental waterway. This adds to and replenishes their skills, schemas, talents and experiences. When you jump back into the cycle of learning, growing and leading, you always start off at a higher level. Why? Because you aren't starting from scratch, you're starting from experience. The key to success from there forward is to recognize, appreciate and apply all of the gains you made along the way. Continue playing the game, but ensure that you're always first and foremost a fan.

LISTEN, COACH

"The core is just always those relationships, building those relationships. Finding out what it is that you have in common, what you do differently, finding those strengths and weaknesses. For me, I have to find out 'What is my supporting role?' That makes me really solid on what my focus and my mission is."

THERESA CRNKOVICH, KANSAS STATE UNIVERSITY

Much like how in the Offense, Defense and Everything Else chapter I said you have to think big and then in the Team Captains chapter I said you have to think small, now I'm going to tell you that even though I just said you have to be a leader, now I'm going to say you need to be a listener. It's a mind cluster, I know. This is how my brain works. It's also how business works.

It might seem counterintuitive to read a book about the workplace and not travel through it in chronological order—first I was advising you to learn how to lead and *now* I'm morphing into advising you on how to *be led*—but I assure you that there is indeed a method to my madness. In fact, there are three reasons why I've organized the text in a seemingly backwards way.

First, it's really important to recognize what good leadership looks like so that you can align yourself with that and not some alternative model. It's also important for you to realize that you can seek out a company that cares about its products from the inside out. These are the organizations that exude a workplace culture, the ones that make their people spring out of bed in the morning or gear up for the late shift. The ones that make people proud to say they work there. The ones where either nobody leaves as the company expands or if they do leave, it's because they're specifically recruited due to their affiliation with that strong company.

These are *leading* companies. Go there. Work within a culture of care, not a culture of quotas! I'm not bashing quotas—they're important and can be achieved. *But* they're easier to achieve within a culture of care. Just think of the example I've already shared of my biggest internal competitor in the sales department. In the end, we shared, we cared, we collaborated and we encouraged each other. Everyone and everything improved, including our sales results. That's good culture.

Second, assuming you buy into the fact that a leader should be your personal ambassador and biggest fan, your mindset already has you better-positioned to grow from anything they can teach you. You're a sponge! Like the leader who told me I needed to look for solutions, good leaders are there to be supportive, to recognize your small and large wins, to set expectations and to provide feedback. This is crucial to realize, because being in a good work environment with good leadership at all levels is exactly *half* of the equation of a good working relationship, no matter whether those people are your bosses, subordinates, cubicle mates or remote colleagues. The other half of the healthy workplace equation is my next point (and the point of this whole chapter). Now it's time for the finger to point at...*you.*

The third reason we're working backwards from future is because there is a 100% chance that you—yes *you*—will be called to do just what you do. (Which is a very old but appropriate cheer.) That is, to be a leader at any given moment and at all steps and stages of your workplace journey. It's important to be ready for that moment whenever, wherever and however it occurs. You'll always have little opportunities to impress others in a positive way: to be a mentor, to inject your unique skills, to be the person who always shows up, to treat all others respectfully, to thoughtfully craft how you choose to use your voice. Especially and most importantly, there will always be an opportunity for you to *listen.* If you do it well, you'll be noticed, because by all measures, you'll be unique. Unlike my cat, who perks up at every creak in the house (my dog, not so much), humans are not particularly good listeners. Furthermore, even though we naturally realize that listening effectively is very important, for some reason, most people don't actually feel a strong need to improve their own skill level. (Spitzberg, 1994) I will tell you with confidence that they—and we—are going about it all wrong.

Although listening and memory recall are notably different, a fun fact relates to both. Did you know that we only remember 25% of what we hear? 25%! Listen—no really, *listen*—there's a slightly overstated myth that we only use 10% of our brains, but whether that's true or false (false, by the way; it's a proven myth), I know that we have the capacity to hold on to more of those soundwaves, and the key to that is to actively *listen.* Aside from our untapped brain potential and all of the interesting stories and information we're missing out on, Harvard University professor and famed negotiator William Ury says that "Listening may be the golden key that opens the door to human relationship." Gosh, that door must be enormous and covered with glitter.

I'm going to be transparent here and admit that for ages—at least four decades—I believed I was a good listener. But after some studying, some roleplay, some brackish-water moments and a few how-to videos, it turns out that I'm not. I'm actually a pretty bad listener. I blame sleep deprivation, and for that I blame blue light but really, it's all my fault and it's just an undeveloped skill. I'm working on it.

So how do I know I'm a bad listener? Perhaps more relevantly, how do you know if *you're* making the cut or not? Well, despite my belief that I generally have polished social skills and polite etiquette, listening and *active* listening are different. That last one is the good stuff! Active listening is far more intentional and results in far better memory recall. Not for nothing, I've also found that it results in far better relationships, as suggested by Professor Ury. This is good for the workplace. It's also good for every person-to-person interaction on any given day!

Interestingly, until recently, I had worked on honing this skill in some parts of my life while totally neglecting it in others. I've come to realize that the last place I learned to actively listen was in my workplace. In that setting, I'd so often been anxious to show and tell a particular narrative so that I could be seen and heard and recognized for my abilities! But again, being *heard* and being *listened to* are not synonymous. If I had spent more time listening and subsequently developing more thoughtful workplace relationships, perhaps my own words would have fallen on more eager ears and I would have arrived at my destination sooner. Not that I'm complaining—I'm learning and reflecting and hoping to pass on a few things to others who could benefit from my experience.

In cheerleading, the art of active listening perhaps comes a little more intuitively than it does in the workplace. Possibly because if you don't do it, you can crash and break your neck. That's the bad news. The good news is that neck-breaking is a lot less likely to happen if you actively listen. That's a little draconian, perhaps, but I'm convinced that active listening is a behavior that happens *only* with intentional practice. We all should consciously work on enhancing our ability to do it well! Luckily, on the court or on the field or wherever your color-coordinated shoes might take you, active listening is ignited by some fairly obvious cues, such as someone shouting "Ready?" and everyone else responding "Okay!" or when the pep band's lead drummer counts in a song with four beats to set the tempo. (Even to this day when I hear four drum beats in a row, my head goes straight to a little "Go-fight-win!" bit we would do between plays.)

In friendships and in more intimate settings, poor listening skills can lead to failed relationships. Unfortunately, in the workplace—where breaking up is much harder than it is in social relationships—underdeveloped skills of any kind, including listening, often just lead to something even worse than failed employment: they lead to stagnation. The subsequent negative effect on your life will happen more slowly and will be less obvious than it is in other settings. It's like being a boiled frog. That's not another Mark Twain quote—it's an apologue that describes a problem that only gets worse until it becomes catastrophic. In other words, if you spend a lifetime not really listening to others around you, you are doomed to fail. Sorry, but sometimes we need a little radically candid straight talk coupled with our active listening.

Active listening opens the door to genuine connections with other people. It's a learned activity and it takes practice, but done well, it's meaningful and mindful and it builds trusting relationships. Several experts have whittled down key characteristics of active listening. While they're all similar in structure and content, in consolidating their commentary, I'll say that active listening moves beyond just polite eye contact and head nods to overall body posture, vocal cues, reflective questioning, validation and most of all, a keen focus on the speaker. If you are actively listening, you are not telling your story or expressing your opinion. Not here. Not now. Try it with intention, and you'll see that active listening is far different from just listening. If you have a spare moment, head over to YouTube and take an active listen to William Ury's talk at TEDxSanDiego. (Heck, while you're at it, listen to his TEDxMidwest talk as well—he's phenomenal.) In his San Diego talk, he says that active listening prevents conflicts before they even start. It's true. It's a game changer. It also makes everything and everyone infinitely more interesting.

We are all highly charged. We care deeply about our work, our reputation and our opinions. Sometimes it's very difficult to step back from that amazing energy and let someone else do the talking while we listen. Correction: *actively* listen. If you practice this skill, however, and combine it with the reflection and mindfulness that we talked about in the Buckets & Candlesticks chapter, you'll be amazed by both what you hear and what you remember. You'll likely also be amazed by what you think and how you grow your skills and your network.

This is where all of the listening and leading come together in this chapter on coaching! Coaches need to collect *all* of the data, assess *all* of the risks and rewards, and consider *every* angle and *every* opportunity in order to set the best goals, give the best direction and call the best plays. They can't possibly be effective without all of that information. Fortunately, business trends are on the side of leading from within, and if modern leadership and innovation have taught us one thing, it's that crowdsourcing works. Talking with and listening to your team at every level of the organization works. Intrapreneurship works, so long as there's a leader who can set aside crusty, musty philosophies and attitudes towards being the top dog and lean into their stakeholders instead.

If you're skeptical about this for any reason, check out the story or film on Flamin' Hot Cheetos® and then tell me I'm wrong. You'll see that listening is leading and leading is listening. The best leaders have a learner's mindset, so don't think of it as a one-or-the-other proposition. Becoming the coach or the leader is not a singular stage in your career path or a title to procure. And don't sweat being the subordinate who's taking direction and following a plan when you're anxious and ready to grow in your workplace or when you're consciously stepping aside to cheer on someone else's good work. Take every moment as a learning opportunity by listening to the people around you at every level of the organization. You might just hear something that changes your life and sets you up for that next teachable, coachable opportunity.

READY? OKAY!

"I'm like, 5, 6, 7, 8, let's go!"

NICOLE ROLLINS, UNIVERSITY OF MEMPHIS

You might not have heard the latest scoop, but Monster.com still exists! I'll pause here for a moment of silence to give thanks for their magical matchmaking between my career path and me way back at the turn of the century.

Still pausing. Still thankful.

[Crickets…]

Okay, I'm back. If you were listening or reading carefully, you'll note that I casually mentioned Monster.com twice before already, so it's a little redundant. However, it's clearly a big deal to me, so I'm making the point one last time because it's important to give thanks. You know what else is important? Looking out for your peeps, yo! Your partners in crime, your office buddies, your work spouses (I read recently that this term is on the outs for some reason; not sure why), your team. It's not just important for the quality of your work, either, in fact. Which comes full circle here, as posted on Monster. com: "89% of workers say work relationships matter to their overall quality of life." They also say that "work friendships make employees more productive." The net-net is that having a good relationship at work is very, very important! And net-net is a true and final result, so you know I'm serious.

Let's be pragmatic and talk about partnerships and teamwork using a broad brush. In the context of physical fitness, partners make you feel more motivated and focused. In an investment setting, partners minimize risk and help leverage each other's experiences. In the worst of times—we're talking wartime here—partners ensure that nobody surprises you when you're not looking. The latter instance is where the phrase "I got your back" comes from, actually.

In a lighter context, in cheerleading, partners can very literally lift you up when you are down and help you achieve new heights. Besides the fact that the last sentence could be printed out on a Cricut Maker® machine with fancy foil paper and transferred to a YETI® mug, partnerships require important work.

In collegiate cheerleading programs of all shapes, sizes and stages, people build stunts. Remember the shoulder stands? Well, stunts are serious stuff—they fail and sometimes people get injured. Not because anyone means to do harm, but because someone isn't giving their 100% to the moment. It could be the base (the person on the bottom), or maybe the flyer (the person on top) or perhaps the spotters (the final line of protection). It could also be the coach if they're not making wise choices. No matter who, somebody did or didn't do something that resulted in a misfire.

This is why partnerships are not ever a 50/50 proposition—they're a 100/100, all-in-by-both-parties kind of deal. Why? Because in cheerleading and everywhere else, if your partner is not giving it their all, they can throw you off course, make you look weak, step all over you or drop you and tarnish your image.

Similarly, when we're hyper focused on what everyone else is doing without applying a little self-examination, we can get sloppy. I've seen this in others and I've experienced it in myself. In cheerleading, I once spaced out on a high-stakes basket toss that could have cost me my life. It didn't, as you can read, but I was lucky. That space-out did, however, cause me to spend a night in the hospital and a few weeks in a neck brace. I didn't only set myself back in confidence, I significantly upset my partners. Everyone in that situation was hurt, either physically or emotionally. I learned very quickly that I needed to be more present going forward.

In the workplace, where presumably everyone has their feet on the ground or at least where you're grounded in a certain task, you have the opportunity to reap all of the benefits of partnerships without risking a catastrophic neck injury. However, you still have to give 100% and similarly expect it from your peers. And don't even think that if you give 100%, the other person or people will give far less and you'll get stuck with all of the work and only half of the credit. That's so pre-career! You're serious now, and so are most of the people around you.

Don't underestimate your colleagues. Align yourself with go-getters, and they will get going. And then *you'll* get going and then *they'll* get going some more and then *you* some more…and then *everyone* will be soaring in the workplace! It's true. Then and only then will you be able to see the real growth: growth in performance and growth in outcomes. It won't just be you standing around doing your thing, you'll be *building* something. Building a culture. Building momentum. Building a company. Building an enterprise!

So are you ready? Okay! Then get ready for this: there's something fancy and exciting called the Pygmalion effect. It's based on a 1968 research study in which teachers told students they had high expectations for them because they were basically so extra. Guess what? They *were* so extra because their teacher said so and they believed it and then they outperformed themselves. Here's how they wrap it up at the George Lucas Educational Foundation: "Positive expectations influence performance positively, and negative expectations influence performance negatively." Pretty straightforward!

So set expectations high for yourself and for the people around you. You'll begin to see the positive momentum right away, and momentum is critical. You'll recall from Making the Other A-Team chapter the saying that if you aren't growing, you're dying. While I still don't love that quote, it's momentous and it still works. (Coincidentally, I feel the same way about coffee.) The workplace is a sophisticated mechanism. It's part artificial intelligence, with emotionless structured learning capabilities, and part wild kingdom, all full of wonder and creativity and possibility. And true to both of those parts, it's always growing. If you're not growing with it, you can get swallowed up by the vines just like Dwayne Johnson's character in *Jungle Cruise*.

When we aren't performing at our best, our colleagues will find work-around solutions to advance themselves, their objectives and their projects, thereby leaving us in the dust. This happens when we don't have good partners and when we haven't aligned ourselves with true leaders…but mostly this happens when we don't have a positive growth mindset. When we see this happening to others, we need to flex our own leadership skills and build those individuals back up and cheer them on for the(ir) greater good. But we need to be especially astute at noticing when it's happening to ourselves and realize the best that can come of lackluster participation in the workplace is lackluster partnerships and performance. If we let ourselves down, by default, we let our partners down. So stay focused. Stay in the game. Stay ready, okay?

FUMBLES & SPIRIT STICKS

"The biggest moments of growth are always those most challenging, difficult times when you handle them properly."

HEATH PERRY, KANSAS STATE UNIVERSITY

W e touched on this briefly in the last chapter, but let's be real and accept that some days aren't our best. We're not feeling well, we didn't get much sleep, we had a falling-out with someone we care about, some unforeseen incident negatively affected our day… And now we're at work. And we're in a mood. And we… fumble. Who do we take it out on?

You're expecting me to say "the people we love" or "those we care most about." But no. It's quite simply whoever is around us. It's true that by the numbers, the people we love the most are *around* us the most, but bad moods are total opportunists and will lash out at whomever is nearest: our cubicle mate, our team, our conference call attendees, our partners. It's not necessarily the people we're closest to in spirit, it's the people we're closest to in proximity. And mind you, when we lash out or give off negative vibes, we are not giving 100%.

I've definitely lost my composure in the workplace, and it's never been pretty. I've also made bad choices and acted inappropriately and unintentionally! One time, I shared office gossip that I swore I'd keep secret…and it came back around to bite me in less than an hour. Interestingly, I broke a tooth that day and ended up needing a crown. I've always thought that was some sort of divine intervention payback. That year and every year since, I've given up gossip for Lent!

Another time I was attempting to multitask while on a conference call and didn't realize that my phone was not on mute. Oops… And in possibly my worst *ever* workplace fumble, I once very accidentally placed my rather brilliant boss in a negative light in an email to our company's most important partner…aaaand I copied her on it. Darn you, poor choices! And darn you, auto-populate!

Fumbles hurt, but they're human and they happen. There's no choice but to find a way forward even though a heapin' helpin' of self-loathing might occur. So when fumbles do happen, how do you move on? How do you hang on to that ball despite foul weather, a bad pass or a line of defenders and ensure that your partnerships and relationships will continue to operate at a high level of positivity at all times? Well, first off, humble and sincere apologies certainly help. But second, take a note out of the cheerleader's playbook and fake it 'til you make it with a big toothy smile!

Cheerleaders are typecast as perpetually peppy people, but you need to know that they are every bit as human as the next person. They wake up every day and put their bloomers on one leg at a time. However, the very nature of their sport gives them an emotional advantage over others without the participants even realizing it. It's not the hours upon hours of exercise and stretching and good cardiovascular health. It's not the inside scoop on all the players and coaches and knowledge of the game(s) and all the travel perks. It's not even the courtside seats that makes them winners. Nope. In fact, it's far more simple than that: it's their smile. Yes, it's part of the job, but it's also a huge benefit on and off the court, and you can bet I'm overcome with joy to share that the smile's secret sauce literally has a first name. And no, it isn't O-S-C-A-R. It's neuropeptides.

Literally, the teeny-tiny molecules that are released when our smile muscles contract have the word "pep" right in 'em. Coincidence? I think not. Those little peppy molecules in turn trigger the dopamine, serotonin and endorphins that make us happy. It's true! "When our smiling muscles contract, they fire a signal back to the brain, stimulating our reward system and further increasing our level of happy hormones, or endorphins." I grabbed that specific quote from Ding Li, the winner of FameLab's most talented young science communicator. (I bet she's a happy person!) That said, while her speech on the topic and her research were award-winning, the concept is not novel. The theory was first presented in Charles Darwin's facial feedback hypothesis and has been proven to be true over and over again since then. The best part (aside from your own mental wellness) is that a smile will rub off on the people around you. Yawns also rub off on the people around you, but we're not trying to bring ourselves and our colleagues down, so we'll stick to smiling. Smiling conveys a message that you're happy and relaxed and will therefore have a direct positive effect on your peers and colleagues. So even if you are in the mood of all moods, take one for the team and smile! Like it or not, you'll be happy in a matter of seconds and so will everyone around you. This is what I like to call "passing the spirit stick."

In cheerleading, the spirit stick has power, real and true power. Everybody wants the spirit stick! The best thing about it is that everybody has an equal chance of earning it. You don't have to be the most talented or the loudest. You don't have to have the best presentation or be a member of the best team. You don't have to be a company or industry veteran or have the most tenure. What you *do* have to have is enthusiasm. You have to cheer as much—if not more—for others as you do for yourself. You have to lift people up emotionally, be their fan and leave them better than you found them. You have to try your hardest and give your best to your partners and to all you do, and you have to do this over a sustainable period of time.

Everyone wants the spirit stick because it speaks to your character, and that's something you can have throughout all of time. You can have it on your first day of work as much as you can have it on your last day of work. You can have it every day in between. And it all starts with choosing your attitude and putting on that happy face!

Your ability to avoid the big fumbles and self-correct those down days with simple techniques like smiling will attract others to you and your work. You'll become a go-to person for solving challenges and chasing opportunities because people will find you generally approachable. When that happens, you grab that spirit stick and you make sure that everyone around you feels your positive energy! Beware, however. The rule in cheerleading is that the spirit stick can't hit the floor—that's just bad luck, the worst. The only way to let it go is to pass it on to someone else to carry. This is mentorship. This is leading by example. This is trusting the people around you.

You should always want the spirit stick, you should always *be* the spirit stick, but most of all, you should always strive to pass it on.

GAME DAY

PRE-GAME

"Whether it's continuing with something that you're already good at or it's adjusting to new parameters, you really want to take what you learned from previous interactions, positive or negative, and make adjustments before the next one in order to increase your effectiveness."

JASON EAGAR, TEXAS CHRISTIAN UNIVERSITY

This is it: game day. You've arrived and you're ready *and* you've got the spirit, yes you do! Game day is huge, and it starts well before the whistle blows. In the world of sports and in the workplace, we're all players and the game is always on. You can tag in and tag out, you can switch from offense to defense, you can change teams, you can even have a time-out or an off season, but the career game is ongoing and we're all playing an instrumental part. Whether we're in the spotlight or operating the spotlight, the game wouldn't and doesn't happen without each of us doing our jobs and tending to our responsibilities. We all play a position and a role. We represent a team, a department, an organization, an industry. Most of all, we represent ourselves.

Until this point in our lives, we've focused on the long game. We attended tryouts and conducted practice run-throughs. We earned certifications and degrees and seniority or tenure and worked our way to a place where we're being trusted to carry out important work. The long game places a focus on us and our growth and development, and that's a good thing. It's what keeps us going as we see ourselves making progress and it's what keeps us from getting benched along the way because we're working to remain at the top of our game.

During this stage, it's important and okay to focus on yourself first because you'll need that self-awareness, experience and wisdom to guide you in the direction of your strengths and values and away from your weaknesses and/or tempting-but-short-term opportunities. The long game is so critical that I've dedicated two out of the three sections of this book, Tryouts and Practice, to discussing it.

However, there comes a time when the ball is in your hands (thank you, awesome leader who passed that ball!) and the pace of work picks up. So far, your whole career life has been centered around you and what you have to offer. That's normal—it's part of the developmental process. But now you can think critically and process complex ideas quickly, and that's a game changer and a career jumping-off point. You're no longer working paycheck to paycheck. You're no longer thinking of business exclusively in terms of seasons, product launches, sales quotas or weekly cycles. You are at and in the height of the daily grind. This is minute-to-minute work combat, and you'll need all of that long-game experience and confidence to help you make on-the-fly decisions that are good and that help you be the person who so calmly took in the emotions and needs of an angry buyer and thoughtfully responded. That time has come, and it's called game day. Welcome to the short game!

In cheerleading, game day is of course a showcase for talent. Everyone shows up with their best self on game day, and I mean *everyone*. It's not just the cheerleaders—it's also the fans, parking attendants, program hawkers, stadium electricians and every person on and off the field. Each and every one of them brings their long-game experience to get the job done against a countdown clock. But there's something different about *this* day that isn't the same as the last game day nor the next game day, and that difference is your opposition. On *this* day, you have to think about what specific other people have to offer. And you only really need to think about that for a finite period of time.

So how do you prepare for that moment? You pre-game. And by pre-game, I don't mean you snarf up those last few pigs in a blanket or gulp down your beverage. I mean you cram.

Wait, what? How is cramming a good thing? I know—it feels like such a dirty word! Some argue that cramming is no good because crammed information is situated only in your short-term memory. (Along with all of those things you heard but didn't listen to.) That pretty much sums up my counterargument for why cramming is not *no* good but *so* good. I don't have a problem with short-term memory because as we discussed earlier, the real work comes through reflection and metacognition. Also, some things truly do only require a moment of our focus, like a game, a convention, a sales pitch or a customer experience.

Another good thing about cramming: it stresses you out. That's also a good thing. Again, I know! This chapter is a conundrum, but trust me, stress is good. Also trust the award-winning psychologist and teacher Kelly McGonigal, who said, "Stress can energize you and help you focus." We like that. We need that. And *that*…helps us succeed at the short game.

Athletes prepare for the short game in the pre-game process by reviewing tape to learn the moves and plays of the individuals who are opposing them. They do this in the few days and moments leading up to the game and then not again unless or until they are matched up against that same opponent. Not to get ahead of myself, but to share something related that we'll talk more about later, after the game, the athletes review tape or film again. At *that* stage, they're checking out their own moves and plays and evaluating their own performance highs and lows. But more on post-game later. For now, all you need to know is that you can metaphorically review your own film, too!

In the absence of professionally edited video, when you prepare for your opponent in the workplace, the easiest way to pre-game is to ask your peers who have already done it *exactly how they did it* and also what they would do more of or differently. That's it. That's the workplace pre-game—it's reviewing the tape with a human connection. (Bonus for active listening!) It's simple, it's effective, and even though you only need your colleague's advice for the short game, that moment of interaction will stick with you (and possibly them) for the long haul. Make those connections, ask those questions, picture the potential scenarios unfolding in your head like a film and prepare yourself. Most importantly, realize the value of those short-duration, pre-game connections you're making and don't squander them. Realize that almost all athletic game days involve contact sports and create that metaphor in the workplace. There's no emailing on game day, not on the court and not in the office. You go *to* the person *in* person. See them with your eyes and not just your ears. If proximity is an issue, pick up the phone. Make contact.

I'll tell you a story. When I was working in a sales capacity, I was given a geographic territory of relative importance. I reached out to all of my new buyers with a very personal and individualized email. I introduced myself and made sure I let them know how important they were to me and how I hoped to be a value-add to their business. I wrapped up my email by asking when a good time would be for me to call. I meant it, too—I was excited about the job and my new relationships. But guess what? Nobody responded. Literally not *one* person. Nobody responded even though I was selling something they wanted and needed.

Even though this was a few years after the incident where I focused only on myself during a job interview, there I was again, focusing only on myself and on making my job easy and seamless. What can I say? Sometimes professional growth is slow! But while that wasn't a shining moment on my historical employment record, it was a great opportunity for me to listen to feedback. You can probably guess what my amazing and honest boss so candidly said when I told him about the situation: "Pick up the phone."

I hadn't stopped to think that my buyers were busy in their own capacity and received oodles of emails from people just like me every day. I hadn't stopped to review their unique business models or operating styles to find out how they liked to be contacted, what their staffing situation looked like, when they conducted most of their purchases and so on. Just like I knew team records back in my cheerleading days, I knew the totality of the buyers' business with our company, but I didn't know the kind of details I would have known if I had really studied the buyers or if I had simply asked the previous territory manager or my boss for insight.

There's some irony in the fact that gaining more experience in the workplace is what ultimately taught me that asking for help is the optimal business tactic. I was too busy trying to prove that I could do everything the best and I wasn't humble enough to do it right the first time by reviewing the tape. As a former public relations professional, I was confident in my writing skills, so I defaulted to them in my sales capacity. But some things that look good on paper don't actually pan out in real life, like trying to move from the top of a two-and-a-half-person-high pyramid to a tumble pass in less than an eight-count. Cheerleading reference there.

But picking up the phone, knocking on the doors, meeting for lunch… those are the workplace strategies that result in a home game advantage. They're the equivalent to the Voice of the Wildcats saying— in a long, strung-out, but enthusiastic way—"Let's get ready to RUUUUMMBLE!" Those personal tactics are what you do to get to know someone or an organization even before you try to assure them of your winning expertise. That assurance indeed comes next, but before you get that W, be sure to review the tape and make those connections. Without doing so, you're just another player.

RULES OF THE GAME

"I don't remember much from the first tryout except that every single guy who showed up made it."

ERIK MORRISON, UNIVERSITY OF DELAWARE

The bell just rang and cramming time is over. Time to be put to the test! For those of us who agree with Woody Allen (controversies aside) that 90% of success is just showing up, there's a good chance that we will indeed do well. I love that mindset and enthusiastically embrace it, but specifically only when using a macro lens. Consistently showing up, stepping up, raising your hand and taking the ball will definitely lead to wins throughout your career. But will they lead to a win today? Who knows. You might predict a positive outcome, but predictions are really only a mixture of part guess and part preparation. One thing that's certain is that nobody goes into a game knowing exactly how it will end.

Upsets happen all the time. Given the drama inherent in a word like "upset," you'd think it would only be a random occasion, but jump on YouTube and type in "greatest upsets" and see what you get. I mean, it's exorbitant. Someone needs to better define the term or build in some criteria, for goodness' sake! Where's the filter? Not surprisingly, all of the YouTube videos pertain to sports upsets, but I've seen some impressive workplace upsets as well, like when Cirque du Soleil all but ousted the Ringling Bros. and Barnum & Bailey circus. Like when mobile phones took the place of pocket cameras. Like when ride shares such as Uber and Lyft displaced taxi cabs. Like when Target joined the ranks of the Big Three toy retailers (Wal-Mart, K-Mart and Toys "R" Us) and shortly thereafter K-Mart entered a death spiral, as did many big-box stores and ultimately shopping malls.

There have also been some near misses like the Y2K bug, when those of us already in the workplace at the time used hundreds of thousands of dollars of our operating budgets to secure our technology from the doomsday effects of moving from "99" to "00." I mean, people were freaking out! Aaaannd it ended up being no big deal. Honestly, the only time people considered partying like it was 1999 was when the year turned from 1998 to 1999. By the time New Year's Eve 1999 *did* roll around, we'd forgotten to party—we were all waiting by our computers, anxious to see if they'd start or if all of our information would be missing or stolen. It was crazy for sure, but guess what? We were prepared, just in case. And that's what you need to be, too! You want to be two parts prepared for any outcome when whipping up your predictions. Tip the odds of success in your favor by using what you learned about emotion regulation from the Buckets & Candelsticks chapter, and being extra everything on your big day. This big day! Whether you're in your car, on a train or a plane or already walking through the door, you're on your way. *This* is the time to think like all athletes, cheerleaders or otherwise.

Athletes have a number of things in common, but one of the quirkiest and yet most relevant to this book is that they're superstitious. In cheerleading, as you know, you can never drop the spirit stick. Ever. For all of time. Serious stuff. But on game day, before you even run out of the tunnel and into the spotlight, take a moment to meditate, say a prayer, touch a logo or lapel or don a specific pair of socks or bloomers if that's your thing. Do something that you can return to if you lose focus for even one tiny moment.

Superstitious rituals lead to preparedness. They lessen inconsistency and increase regularity. In the workplace, they take the shape of going to bed on time, eating good meals, showing up early, reviewing your plan and executing with perfection. You've done those things and you're ready to roll! All that remains is a little pep talk to go over the rules of the game, so let's do that.

Rule Number One: *Put your game face on*. In cheerleading, this is the smile we talked about. It's not only good for your soul, it's good because it gives you a look of confidence that proves to others that you represent the team and that you are *ready*. You plaster on that game face and you take it with you out your door and everywhere you go that day. You take it with you when you meet with the buyers, the early adopters, the influencers and the supporters. You take it with you as you listen to their stories and let them know that you share their ideas and values. You take it with you to the warm-up room, where you connect with your peers and partners and assure them of your focus and readiness. And without a *doubt*, you take it with you to the showdown as you face your competition and your judges.

Rule Number Two: *Be your own hype girl*. What comes out of your mouth goes back into your ears, so if you know one thing right now, it's that you are ready, willing, able and winning! You were made for this moment 100%. For the sake of expanding my target audience, I'll provide a Kenny Rogers reference from my early career days. If you've never treated yourself to his song "The Greatest," do so now. It's as good for the soul as a smile is for your face. Listen to his music. Listen to any music or advice that builds you up and then go out there and crush it.

Rule Number Three: *Drink the Kool-Aid.* Hydration is good, and so is filling yourself with your team spirit. Head to toe, you've got to be the brand, be the professional, and be so sure of yourself that you can't lose! In cheerleading, we have uniforms and pom-poms, temporary tattoos and ribbons. But so do the fans, the players, the coaches and everyone working or attending the event. The real differentiator when it comes to cheerleaders is our spirit and our position on the field. It is literally a cheerleader's job to get the audience to get into the game, and that's your job at work, too, so drink it in!

Rule Number Four: *Know your audience and speak the language.* You've talked to yourself; now you need to talk to others. In cheerleading, there's a stunt where the base stands tall and holds both of the flyer's feet above their head in one hand. It looks fairly simple, but in actuality, it's not. Where I cheered, this is called a Cupie. In other places, it's called an Awesome. Same move, different name, very different culture. Wherever you are, you need to speak the language of both your organization and your audience. What you share with them is both a representation of your unique selling proposition and an understanding of their needs and cultures.

Rule Number Five: *Get open.* Put yourself in a position to get the spotlight and be seen and be heard. Then make the play. Pay attention to what's going on around you. Actively listen. Find out where people are with their thoughts and actions and what could transpire in the next few moments. And be ready and willing to seize opportunities. One thing's for sure: you're not going to get any opportunity if you're not open to it. So get open!

Rule Number Six: *Make it a slam dunk.* You showed up, you're taking every opportunity and you are going to deliver with enthusiasm. But don't just give them what they want, give them what they want and *more.* Give them a slam dunk! When this moment comes to an end, be sure you've left the crowd with something that will make them go wild, something that will make them remember your name and support your brand. Always overdeliver.

Rule Number Seven (there has to be a Rule Number Seven because we're superstitious): *Thank your fans and the audience for showing up.* It might feel like it's all about you right now because we're actually talking all about you and how you can be great in the workplace, but it really is all for the fans. You've got to make your boss, your buyers, your stakeholders, your peers and your colleagues into your biggest fans, and the best way to do that is by showing your appreciation for their time and efforts. You didn't get to where you are by being a solo artist. Whether it's natural or not, you're a team player and you need to show some love.

Those are the rules of the game. If you're going to win, abide by them! Everyone in the workforce is playing the same game, yet you'll no doubt encounter people who don't play by the same rules. Just remember: although people who don't play by the rules can indeed win the most, they'll never win it all. Eventually, they'll foul out!

BE AGGRESSIVE

"Every job I've taken, I've taken with the assumption
that I would do that job for the rest of my life,
so that I would do everything I could to make
it successful and so that if I ever left, I would
leave it in good standing for whomever came
next. That's always been my view. I've always
taken a job where I thought there was something
I could add and something I could learn."

JOEL LEHMAN, UNIVERSITY OF ILLINOIS

O n the surface, aggressiveness—much like stress—gets such a bad rap in the workplace. This is incredibly curious, because during all of our early and pre-adult developmental years and all of the trials and errors and testing out of what we like and dislike, the advice that rings most clearly in my memory is that if we really wanted something, we needed to go after it. In other words, we need to be aggressive. It's also probably *the* most well-known cheer by cheerleaders and non-cheerleaders alike. Can't you just hear it now? "Be. Aggressive. B.E. Aggressive. B.E.A.G.G.R.E.S.S.I.V.E. Aggressive!!"

As far as I can tell, that never meant anything negative—it just always implied that you need to go after the things you want. To find a way to achieve your goals.

In cheerleading, you can never go into a stunt and come out the other side of it in good condition without being very intentional and deliberate about where you want to end up. There are simply too many twists and turns and jumps and bumps along the way that you have to endure. If you aren't completely focused and determined and aggressive about achieving your goal, you're not going to. And stunting aside, you can't lead a crowd without the same aggressiveness, either. You know that's true if you've ever tried to start a wave in a stadium or an arena without the help of modern scrim boards. We're talking the old-fashioned way. You can't just pop your arms up into the air and expect the wave to ensue. It takes much more deliberation than that. You have to first rally the people around you and tell them about your plan. You have to get the early adopters and your friends and fans to follow along. You have to throw your arms up and maybe even shout a little, saying something intentional like, "Hey, everyone! Let's do the wave!" You might even have to do it multiple times in short succession before enough people start to notice and you get even the slightest hint of momentum. It's hard! You have to really put yourself out there—you have to care a little less about what people might think at that moment and stay focused on your goal. It takes some aggression, but that's *not* a bad thing. The workplace is no different. However, unlike on game days when there's an expectation and untethered acceptance of said hurling-arm-toss behavior, in the workplace, it helps to camouflage your aggression with a little bit of finesse.

Most of us have likely encountered a colleague whose aggression clearly put them in the "naughty" bucket of peers, not the "nice" one.

But there are also those colleagues who have gone out on a limb and earned the admiration of others for their bravery, their stick-to-it-ness, their uncompromising moral compass and their determination. Both of these types of people are aggressive in the workplace, but how do we make sure that *we* land in the nice bucket and not the naughty one?

First of all, you can't take prisoners. By that, I literally mean don't take prisoners or shoot people down. Leave everyone standing! Being aggressive in the workplace is not about beating the other team or proving anyone else wrong! Instead, it's entirely about proving yourself worthy of being heard and listened to and trusted. You will in fact get more ear time from others if you make a point of delivering thoughtful opinions that include the slam dunk. It's not just about making a determined statement or sharing the brilliant idea—you need to follow up with a strong case for *why* you're right. And the reason needs to be for the better of your brand and not for the better of you.

Second, choose your battles. Even cheerleading has an off season, as do all sports. You can't be at the top of your game at every game if you're always *in* the game. Think back to the chapter on Team Captains and recall those brackish waters, that development of our personal estuaries and mental ecosystems. Truly, I loved cheering for teams at my alma mater and I love cheering for my colleagues at work, but if I had to do either seven days a week, it would probably get a little stale. Heck, *I'd* probably get a little stale, or worse, injured or just plain cranky. At some point, you need to step back and catch your breath. Give others a chance to join or lead the conversation, to garner new information and perspective and expertise. Then stand out or stick up when it's really necessary and important.

Third and finally, timing is everything! On one hand, nobody's going to join your wave or see your fancy new stunt when the spirit is low. That's a little counterintuitive, right? You might be thinking that *exactly* when the spirit is low is when teams and people need a little cheering up. But you can't go in with pom-poms all awhirl and shouting all the time—sometimes the moment requires a hush over the crowd or a little smooth jazz music from the pep band instead of your fancy-pants jazz hands. Ultimately, you have to learn how to read the room. Not to beat the drum too hard, but…you guessed it: the importance of active listening can't be understated.

On the other hand, some moments are indeed ripe for the picking. There will be times when it's fourth and goal or overtime and tied during a time-out and everyone is looking at you and willing you to raise the roof with a crowd-rousing cheer that will unite everyone with one strong voice. And you've got just the cheer! Those are good moments. And they're special moments—they're not everyday, every-moment moments. Treat them with respect and be grateful for the opportunity to be heard.

LOSING SLUMPS &
WINNING STREAKS

*"Sometimes the goal needs to be adjusted;
if it continually can't be achieved, go
around it and try something else."*

TRACY BAYLIFF, OKLAHOMA STATE UNIVERSITY

Remember back at the beginning when we talked about setbacks and the fact that somebody will always be better than you? Right! Super uplifting, rah-rah kind of chapter. Well, that chapter was about learning from others, staying with your dreams and passions and taking your time to grow and improve. It's part "be patient" and part "engage in some self-realization." But what happens when you've been patient and you've done the growth and development and you've honed your craft and you *still* find yourself in a rut? What happens when the team you're on is the losingest team in the industry? Or worse, the losingest team in *history*? What happens when you didn't get extra shelf space at a retailer, the seed funder didn't like your tech innovation, a homeowner didn't like the design you suggested or the students you've been working with haven't shown any significant improvement? What happens when you just don't really like your job at all but you aren't in a place to make a change?

This might sound truly awful or feel truly awful or actually *be* flat-out awful, but there's literally no cheer for feeling awful, so I'm not going to make one up. Wait a minute…that's not true. I just remembered one. Get up. UP! Off your feet. We know you just can't be beat!

And it's perfect, because this is *game day*, people. Not tryouts, not practice. Game day. This is what you were made for! Remember what Steve Kirkland said back in the Making the Other A-Team chapter? He said, "You just have to stay positive, no matter what happens." And he's right—you just have to.

You've got one job, and that is to get out there and win. Luckily for all of us, winning doesn't always mean winning it *all*—sometimes it just means we've got positive momentum. Charlie Sheen clearly demonstrated this and even created the phrase "Winninggggggg!!" to reflect every little thing that goes right. I'm not suggesting we look to Sheen or anyone else for benchmarking what feels good in any given moment, it's just that little wins are every bit as important as big wins. For example, everybody recognizes the person who never gives up, who rallies the team when they're down, who pushes through to the final buzzer and then goes person to person and says, "Good game!" Everybody respects the person who can identify key learnings from the losing slumps and use them to their advantage at a later date. Everyone knows these people; everyone should strive to curate those qualities and *be* that person.

Think about it: do you know who won the quarter-mile at the last Olympics and did you even see the race? No? But have you seen the video of the track athlete who fell down at the start or lost a shoe and still got up and gave it their all? Or the one where the female runner who's visually impaired is tethered to a sprint guide and absolutely slayed? My eyes have never been more fixated on a person running in circles as they were when I watched those runners. They never gave up, and their efforts get my heart racing even after 20 views on Instagram. You know who else never gave up? Michael Jordan, J.K. Rowling, Walt Disney, Oprah Winfrey, Henry Ford, Helen Keller, Jay-Z, Roberta Gibb, The Beatles, Fred Astaire and Babe Ruth. There's more! Albert Einstein, Ruth Bader Ginsburg, Colonel Harland Sanders, Dr. Seuss, Sarah Jessica Parker, Howard Schultz, Misty Copeland and Jim Carrey and so, so, so many more people who maybe don't grace history books or magazine covers, but they're everywhere. And *you* are one of them.

Perhaps you aren't always the big winner, but in the workplace, little wins go a long, long way. The important thing to remember is there's no giving up, so get up and stay up! Losing slumps happen. And believe it or not, they happen to most if not all people. But you still need to show up and put your best foot forward at all times! I'm not talking about being aggressive all the time, I'm talking about being present, being committed and giving it your all. Your work doesn't just represent your company—it represents *you*. And not only are other people watching, so are *you*. You need to get into your own psyche and go, fight, win!

One of my favorite singsongy cheers in high school was the one that went "Go Lions, go! Do your best. Remember that you're fighting for LHS!" You know what's so great about that cheer? It's about doing your best. It's not about ten more yards, sinking a free throw or pinning someone to the ground. *Doing* your best and *being* the best are

distinctively different, and because this book is about doing generally and consistently awesome things in the workplace and not about
climbing to the tippy-top of the pyramid, I'm going to stand firmly
behind *doing* your best as the key to success.

Forbes agrees, or at least one of their writers does. In Remy Blumenfeld's 2019 Forbes.com article titled "Why 'Doing Your Best' Is A Better Bet than 'Being The Best,'" Blumenfeld points out that winning
arguments and outperforming others isn't the way to shine. More
important is improving on your own personal bests, mastering new
skills and being self-motivated. Doing your best is favored by cor-
porations and quite frankly by your workplace peers. "You may be
driven, but you're still able to collaborate usefully," Blumenfeld writes.
I absolutely love his article because he articulates that success is personal. It's something you define using your own benchmarks, and it
ends with happiness within, not as compared with others.

Plenty of sources acknowledge workplace slumps and talk about how
to recognize them and what to do when you're in one. I recommend
you browse the subject if that's where you are, because slumps come
with emotional baggage. Although I walk a straight line of trying to
stay positive, I can admit that it's not *always* easy and sometimes I
have to plaster that neuropeptide-producing smile on with a little
forced effort.

Still, while I agree with most of what I've found on the topic of
doing your best, what I don't see anyone talking about as much—
and what seems to me to be the most basic position of all—is that
we should strive to be both inspiring *and* inspired. I call this an "I
for an I" concept. Without envy or jealousy, we should be able to
do our best while recognizing the qualities in others that we'd like

to emulate and reflect ourselves or that we'd just like to compliment. If we adopt this "I for an I" outlook, our boat and all boats will rise.

If you can get to a point where you're a lifelong learner who's confident with your own talents and you're simultaneously motivating and humble—a.k.a. inspiring *and* inspired—you are *in the game*. You can even be the sideline person totally awestruck by the twisting walk-up back tuck to hands (a seemingly impossible feat) that you just saw flawlessly executed *and* the peer who leapt to their feet with the loudest cheer and *still* be in the game. You might not be the person who executed the maneuver or individually scored the winning point, but everyone will know that you played a supporting role and they'll start to incorporate you into strategic conversations.

CHEERING FOR
THE COMPETITION

*"We may be on different teams but the truth is,
without each other, no one gets to play the game."*

VALERIE MCDOWELL, HAMPTON UNIVERSITY

This is not fake NASCAR. I am not Ricky Bobby and you are not Cal. Just because someone else is first, you are *not* hence, hereto and therefore last. This is higher-order, big-picture thinking. Lest you think otherwise, I assure you that the workplace is just like a professional sport: the people and pieces are always moving. The athletes, coaches, trainers, grounds crew, tech crew…everyone and everything is always moving. Always. In some ways, there are no teams, just whole industries and whole movements. Like blobs, but the sparkling and iridescent kind. If this were a gardening book, I might say like creeping phlox or bioluminescent beetles captured on long-exposure film. Yeah. That sounds better and more dynamic.

Anyway, the workplace is a whole moving object, and nobody except subject matter experts looks back and says, "That's the time when so-and-so cut the biggest deal ever." No. They say, "Those were the glory days!" Or if you're looking way back, they say, "That was the Stone Age—that was the Classical Era. *This* is the Modern Era." That last one, by the way, is the one we're in, and it has been happening for 200-plus years. It's important that you think about that before you let yourself feel the weight of the world for any one little thing, any one moment in time, any one big play or any opportunity. Like, anything at all, really. You're entitled to your big wins and your heavy topics, but I recommend keeping things in perspective.

In recent and semi-recent times (definitely Modern Era), we've seen workplace examples of everyone moving together in the workplace for better and for worse. Thinking of my own career, I can name a few pivotal moments when I realized it wasn't all about me or even about my company: the dot-com boom and bust, September 11th, the stock market crash of 2008, when gas prices were super low in 2016 and then super high in 2022, the global supply chain crisis. Hello? Covid!

The reality is that there are times when we're all moving together and at the mercy of the stars. During those times, all we can do is cheer for anything and everything that's good. There are also times when there are major industry or cultural shifts. It's easy to immediately think of technology and the trickle-down effect it has on everything else, but shifts happen all the time and in every nook and corner of life. Heck, when I was cheering in high school and in college, big hair was a thing. We're talking smelly chemical perms, teased bangs with hairspray and giant bows on top of our heads. I know you're going to be a little jelly right now, but I did just see an Instagram post from my alma mater, and there's good news: the bows are back, baby! *Bam!* Cultural shift right there for ya, and I did *not* see that one coming but I am well positioned for it. But seriously, shift happens, and it's something you need to keep in perspective, especially when it comes to strategic and long-term planning.

You also need to keep your competition in perspective. Imagine you and your company are at the Rose Bowl parade where everyone has a float or a car or a horse or a place in line. Regardless, you're all in a cluster heading in the same direction, no matter which team is yours or what part you're playing. These are the times when you're cheering for everyone, even the competition. I once heard a speaker who formerly worked at Barnes & Noble say, "We were so busy looking out for Borders that we totally missed Amazon.com." (Another example of a workplace upset!) Think about that. More recently, a friend of mine discussed buying part of a cleaning service. She purchased the industrial linen components (tablecloths, hotel sheets, etc.) but forwent the dry cleaning service. Why? Well, consider that Lululemon stock was $18 per share when it first became available in 2007 and now it's above $300 per share. The workplace is unilaterally more casual than it was at the turn of the century. Athleisure wear has taken off, and you can pretty much wash and dry all of it yourself. Fewer people require the formal workplace attire that used to drive dry cleaning businesses. This is a whole industry being affected. People's livelihoods. Second- and third-generation shops.

When shifts happen, that's when you have to cheer for the competition. Cheer for innovation. Cheer for the people who retool their machines and make them valuable in other ways or the people who take what they've learned and apply it to a new industry. Cheer for the people who look at an existing product and make it fail-safe for the future like all of the orange growers in Florida, Texas, California and worldwide who are fighting citrus greening disease. Cheer for the people who solved the problem that drives your inner passion and yourself to work every day, like figuring out how to deliver unbiased media, engage individuals with disabilities in the workforce, stop the growth of a tumor or teach a child to read.

This is the moment when the injured player on the field finally gets up after all of the onlookers have held their breath for several minutes and you realize how grateful you are just for the game to continue. How grateful you are for the ability to play the game and win… or not win, but still be winninggggggg!!

WINNING IT ALL

"I believe that life is full of little victories and defeats. Some seem larger than others, but winning isn't a goal, it's a mindset. You win if you do your best, give your all, strive to learn more and be better in everything in which you are involved."

MIKE O'HALLORAN, CENTRAL MICHIGAN UNIVERSITY

always found it odd that Queen's anthem, "We Are The Champions," is played after every single major championship game. Have you ever noticed that? Have you ever listened to all of the lyrics, not just the ones that blare "Weeeeeee are the champions, WEEEEEEE ARE THE CHAMPIONS"? I mean, that song—as exhilarating as it is—is about a lifelong battle. It's actually depressing. Freddie Mercury literally says that he's had sand kicked in his face, that it's been no bed of roses, and that we'll keep fighting 'til the end. And this is after the curtain call! *After* "we" became the champions, apparently of the entire flippin' world!

Sure, winning it all happens. It happens all the time, and it's totally sparkly-fingers amazing and worth every piece of confetti cannon shrapnel stuck in your hair and every second of celebrating. But… the tricky part is in identifying, defining and living in the winning moments. Luckily for all of us, only *we* get to define those moments. Nobody else gets to tell us when we've won it all or when we didn't. Nobody else gets to define championship moments as ones that only come after a lifelong battle against all odds.

In the Team Captains chapter, we talked about being a part of the process and leaning in. I suggested that it's not up to any one single other person to raise you up and put you in the game, it's up to *you*. Well, it's also not up to anyone else to decide what it looks like to win. You can celebrate any time you want! In my mind, I won it all because I was a collegiate cheerleader, period. Not because we went to Nationals or sort of went to Nationals. I won it all because I successfully worked with some of the top brands in the world and didn't burn any bridges when I exited those organizations. I won it all when I was offered an amazing job that I hadn't even applied for just because someone else thought I'd be perfect for the position.

Did you notice a thread running through all of that? Those big wins are past-tense wins: I *won* it all, I *was*, I *worked*. So what am I doing now? Well, luckily for me, I'm still winning, and I'm doing it using my own internal metrics. I have a career that offers a real work and home life balance. I have a healthy family structure that I've worked to create through a lot of trial and error. I have the opportunity to try new things and learn from subject matter experts and think creatively during all phases of my workplace experience. That, to me, is winning. All of the little moments. There are atomic habits and there are atomic moments. Remember, little things aren't small.

Realistically, if I use external metrics, I never won it all in cheerlead-ing. I wasn't a master stunter. I got really nervous about my shoes when I was two levels up in the rain. My arms actually don't entirely straighten, and it really shows when I do a high V motion. It was par-ticularly obvious in a picture that included me doing a diamond head stunt that appeared on a "throwback Thursday" Facebook post. Not that I noticed. I had an incredible toe-touch jump that I was super proud of, but something in my ligaments just refused to accept the straddle jump. (It's a different move, I assure you.) Total mystery. I could do an endless number of consecutive back handsprings across the football field and standing back tucks with ease, but not a full from the ground. Our cheerleading team made it to Nationals in San Diego one year and I joined them, but I was on the other A-Team— I was an alternate. The teams we cheered for never won a national championship, either. They were quite good and an insane amount of fun to cheer for, but they never won it "all" if we're talking about the championship ring. But I bet that like me, at least some of them *do* feel like they won it all. And if they're wiser than I am—which is highly likely—then they probably felt that way while they were actu-ally in the moment. I hope so. And I hope you feel that way, too!

To this day, I still identify as a cheerleader, but I'm no longer teth-ered to a single team. Being a cheerleader is a state of mind, a way of being. Also, the memories I made while cheering semi-successfully have actually only gotten sweeter with time. All of them—every last one. I don't have one bad memory to think back on, and it's because I took my own advice from the last chapter and got a little perspec-tive. I feel the same way about my career progression.

Do you have health benefits and are you food- and shelter-secure? Do you have real friends, not deal friends, and mutual respect for your colleagues? Do you know how awesome you are and that if you really want something, it's entirely up to you to go after it and that people are literally cheering for you every step of the way? If you said "yes" to all of those questions, you've *won* it all and you *are still winning*!

I really like what Rakesh Soni has to say in an article he wrote for Forbes.com titled "How Leaders Can Embrace 'Rational Optimism' and Develop a Realistic Plan for Success." In it, he advocates for a leadership style that he calls, as you might have guessed, "rational optimism," which entails remaining committed but also being adaptable. Isn't that such a great metaphor for life in general?

In cheerleading, sometimes even the smallest individuals have to be the base. It happens. Sometimes they have to stay on the ground and flip the sign that says, "Go!" Granted, they have to do it with every ounce of their enthusiasm—you know, a giant step forward with a head bob right as the sign goes up—but it's literally sign-flipping, people. Sometimes the biggest cheerleaders (at my school, these people were all men) have to hold up the school mascot on a palanquin while the zipped-up, masked, fuzzy character does a push-up for every point scored in the game. It's heavy, sucky work, but it's all part of the celebration, and I bet they'd do it all over again today if they could. Likewise, in the workplace, sometimes you have to get the coffee, plan the party, create the presentation deck, crunch the numbers, call the frustrated buyer, rearrange the shelves…rearrange your life.

Whatever happens, whatever choices you make, whatever you do, if you have a winning attitude and the right perspective, if you remain both committed and adaptable, you *will* win it all and you'll be the champion of your own world sans sand in your face.

GAME OVER?

"One thing we emphasize is being a lifelong learner."

AMY STUBBS, KANSAS STATE UNIVERSITY

You've graduated. It's bittersweet. Transitions can be difficult, but sadly there's no avoiding them. And/but—this should be no surprise by now—there's good news! It gets even better!

squeals with delight

You are now in the Alumni Affairs and Development stage! This is the part where you give back your time, treasure and talents. This is your time to choose your level of engagement, attend only the games you want to attend, reflect on all you've accomplished and help others get to the next level, maybe even with a toss-to-hands. This is especially your time to review the other film that we talked about in the Pre-Game chapter, not the one where you're trying to memorize the moves of your opponents. Instead, you're analyzing your *own* performance highs and lows and figuring out what you learned from them and what you can improve upon even further. And what you can do less of and more of and pass on to a new generation.

This is nothing to be upset about! Speaking of which, as much as the term "upset" needs more nuance and boundaries applied to it, the term "learning" needs fewer boundaries. It needs to be infinite and permeative. (I hate to interrupt a serious moment, but honestly, I have to say that I wish I could find a more exciting word than "permeative." It reminds me of gray winter skies that last for months. Rather, I want to portray learning that is far more electric and exciting, like the deafening but glorious sound of waterfowl on a calm lake at dusk in early April.)

Thinking about and analyzing the choices you've made personally and professionally with an outside [of the workplace] perspective will make you more objective, more solutions-oriented and more capable of transmitting what you've learned and accomplished in a variety of contexts. Quite possibly, the best of those ways is through mentorship.

There are oodles of great examples of mentor-mentee relationships! I'll name a few so that you can see that not only are great people mentors, great people are open to *being* mentored. Maya Angelou mentored Oprah Winfrey, Audrey Hepburn mentored Elizabeth Taylor, Steve Jobs mentored Mark Zuckerberg, Steven Spielberg mentored J.J. Abrams, Sir Elton John mentored Lady Gaga and Michelle Robinson mentored Barack Obama (now, *that* was a great pre-game move for both of them!).

In an article on her *Wise Up Networks* blog, Chantelle Argent wrote, "Like Oprah, CEO of PepsiCo Indra Nooyi is another influential woman who sings the praises of the many mentors she has had throughout her life. Nooyi is a massive advocate of mentoring and has said, 'If I hadn't had mentors, I wouldn't be here today. I'm a product of great mentoring, great coaching… Coaches or mentors are very important.'"

Yes! Agreed. And rolling with the positive momentum of this topic, mentorships—like partnerships in cheerleading—are win-win and mutually beneficial. In her article for *U.S. News and World Report* titled "How Mentorship Can Benefit Both the Mentor and the Mentee," Jamela Adam wrote, "Though mentees benefit from mentors' knowledge and guidance, mentors often feel equally rewarded watching their protégés take their teachings and run with them."

Though I think both are critical, it's important to differentiate coaches from mentors. You can be both, but not usually at the same time to the same person. Coaches for the most part provide the plays—they tell you exactly what they're expecting from you. I'm not going to lie, that's sometimes quite nice and very often appreciated by your workplace peers. I love transparency and goal-setting. We need coaches. Mentors, on the other hand, are there to share their experiences and to tell you what they did, for better or worse. They're not necessarily there to tell you what to do. But they do guide you through your unique goals and talents, not theirs. They help you blossom. They're like the best kind of leader, the kind that's your biggest fan.

I hope to be that person and I hope that I am that person. A lot of people say there's a real shortage of mentors stepping into the role since so many baby boomers have retired and some cultural shifts have resulted in more virtual relationships and employees having shorter durations with employers. There's a slew of other reasons, too, but there's a need and it has a human face. If you're at this stage of your career—or even if you're mid-career and have some really cool experience or you're early in your career and can lend an ear and some thoughts to a student—it's all good and necessary and mutually beneficial. Mentorship is a real opportunity for you to shine in the prime time and prove that the game is never really over.

REFERENCES

BUCKETS & CANDLESTICKS

Gross, J. J., & John, O. P. (2003). Individual differences in two emotion regulation processes: Implications for affect, relationships, and well-being. *Journal of Personality and Social Psychology, 85*(2), 348–362. https://doi.org/10.1037/0022-3514.85.2.348

Perrin, A., & Atske, S. (2021, March 26). *About three-in-ten U.S. adults say they are "almost constantly" online.* Pew Research Center. https://www.pewresearch.org/fact-tank/2021/03/26/about-three-in-ten-u-s-adults-say-they-are-almost-constantly-online/

Simon-Thomas, E. R. (2018). *The Four Keys to Happiness at Work.* Greater Good. https://greatergood.berkeley.edu/article/item/the_four_keys_to_happiness_at_work

STANDING OUT

Cherry, K. (2022, October 13). *How Social Comparison Theory Influences Our Views on Ourselves.* Verywell Mind. https://www.verywellmind.com/what-is-the-social-comparison-process-2795872

Littlefield, C. (2019, October 12). *How to Give and Receive Compliments at Work.* Harvard Business Review. https://hbr.org/2019/10/how-to-give-and-receive-compliments-at-work

MAKING THE OTHER A-TEAM

Leonard, B., & Leonard, B. (2014, November 24). *Survey: 23 Percent of Workers Diagnosed with Depression*. SHRM. https://www.shrm.org/resourcesandtools/ hr-topics/risk-management/pages/employees-missed-work-depression.aspx

Mental Health America. (2019). *Depression in The Workplace | Mental Health America*. Mhanational.org. https://www.mhanational.org/depression-workplace

TOSS-TO-HANDS

Heshmat, S. (2019, November 25). *Three Key Elements of Personal Growth | Psychology Today*. Www.psychologytoday.com. https://www.psychologytoday.com/us/blog/ science-choice/201911/three-key-elements-personal-growth#:~:text=These%20 basic%20psychological%20needs%20are

OFFENSE, DEFENSE AND EVERYTHING ELSE

A Broad Perspective: A Must-Have for Promotion. (2021, May 3). Center for Creative Leadership. https://www.ccl.org/articles/leading-effectively-articles/ a-broad-perspective-a-must-have-for-promotion/

TEAM CAPTAINS

Downtime is essential for leadership effectiveness | Peeler Associates. (2012, May 7). Peeler Associates Leadership Perspectives. https://peelerassociates.com/ downtime-is-essential-for-leadership-effectiveness/

TEDx Talks. (2018). We Cannot Lead Others Without First Leading From Within | Lolly Daskal | TEDxLincolnSquare. In *YouTube*. https://www.you- tube.com/watch?v=HGIw1G7Kpgk

LISTEN, COACH

Sheen, C. (2021). *8 inspiring examples of intrapreneurship and employee ideas in action*. Ideas.sideways6.com. https://ideas.sideways6.com/article/inspiring -examples-of-intrapreneurship-and-employee-ideas-in-action

Spitzberg, B. H. (1994). *Effective Listening*. Www.wright.edu. http://www.wright.edu/~scott.williams/LeaderLetter/listening.htm#:~:text=However%2C%20research%20shows%20that%20the

Ury, W. (2015, January 7). *The power of listening | William Ury | TEDxSanDiego*. YouTube. https://youtu.be/saXfavo1OQo

READY? OKAY!

Benefits of Having Affinity Groups at Work. (n.d.). Monster Career Advice. https://www.monster.com/career-advice/article/affinity-group

Solomon, B. (2014, December 16). *The Pygmalion Effect: Communicating High Expectations*. Edutopia; George Lucas Educational Foundation. https://www.edutopia.org/blog/pygmalion-effect-communicating-higher-expectations-ben-solomon

FUMBLES & SPIRIT STICKS

Ding, L. (2014, April 2). *What's the science behind a smile? | British Council*. Britishcouncil.org. https://www.britishcouncil.org/voices-magazine/famelab-whats-science-behind-smile#:~:text=When%20our%20smiling%20muscles%2contract

PRE-GAME

McGonigal, K. (2015). *The Upside of Stress: Why Stress Is Good for You, and How to Get Good at It.* https://digitalwellnesslab.org/parents/young-adults-ages-20-25/

LOSING SLUMPS & WINNING STREAKS

Blumenfeld, R. (2019, April 14). *Why "Doing Your Best" Is A Better Bet than "Being The Best."* Forbes. https://www.forbes.com/sites/remyblumenfeld/2019/04/14/why-doing-your-best-is-a-better-bet-than-being-the-best/?sh=40e2696a7336

R.L. Adams. (2016, September 18). *21 Famous Failures Who Refused to Give Up*. HuffPost; HuffPost. https://www.huffpost.com/entry/21-famous-failures-who-refused-to-give-up_b_57da2245e4b04fa361d991ba

Stibel, J. (2016, August 16). *10 People Who Didn't Give Up*. Bizjournals.com. https://www.bizjournals.com/bizjournals/how-to/growth-strategies/2016/08/10-people-who-didnt-give-up.html

WINNING IT ALL

Soni, R. (2023, February 1). *Council Post: How Leaders Can Embrace "Rational Optimism" And Develop A Realistic Plan For Success*. Forbes. https://www.forbes.com/sites/forbesbusinesscouncil/2023/02/01/how-leaders-can-embrace-rational-optimism-and-develop-a-realistic-plan-for-success/?sh=7544042b6c86

GAME OVER?

Adam, J. (2023, February 24). *How Mentorship Can Benefit Both the Mentor and the Mentee*. U.S. News & World Report. https://money.usnews.com/careers/articles/how-mentorship-can-benefit-both-the-mentor-and-the-mentee

Argent, C. (2020, September 28). *Top 9 Influential People Who Succeeded Because Of Their Mentors*. Wiseup. https://wiseupnetworks.com/blog/top-9-influential-people-who-succeeded-because-of-their-mentors

ABOUT THE AUTHOR

Melinda Carter Oakes is a proud military brat with 14 major geographical moves under her suitcase and briefcase, five of them specifically for her career. Still, she credits Lansing, Kansas as her hometown, the same place where she started earning her stripes as a worker bee and a cheerleader. She is the very essence of a big-hair, bow-wearing, bubbly personality you would expect to be a cheerleader, and she will prove you both right and wrong when it comes to everything you ever thought about cheerleaders.

Melinda began working regularly at the age of 12 and hasn't stopped since. She spent nearly two decades at positions with some of the world's biggest and best brands, including Hallmark Cards, Inc., The Madison Square Garden Company and LEGO Company. She has also worked for cleaning companies and in food service, childcare, printing, ride operations, coaching, home improvement and philanthropy endeavors. She's a workplace scrapper who persevered through blood, sweat and happy tears, and she knows that the keys to success are a positive attitude and a big fan base. Confetti cannons, pompoms and a pep squad also help.

Melinda lives in Ithaca, New York with her husband and two children.